SUCCESS
COMMON
SENSE
— and the —
SMALL
BUSINESS

Patricia Tway, Ph.D.

BETTERWAY BOOKS

Cincinnati, Ohio

Also by Patricia Tway:
People, Common Sense, and the Small Business

Cover design by Rick Britton
Typography by Park Lane Publication Services

97 96 95 94 93   5 4 3 2 1

Library of Congress Cataloging-in-Publication Data

Tway, Patricia
    Success, common sense, and the small business / Patricia Tway.
        p. cm.
    Sequel to: People, common sense, and the small business.
    Includes index.
    ISBN 1-55870-306-3
    1. Small business--Management. I. Title.
HD62.7.T88 1993
658.02'2--dc20   93-4790
                                                                      CIP

*This book is dedicated to my husband,
who made it all possible.*

Acknowledgments

I want to thank the small business owners who agreed to let me describe their experiences. I did not use their names when discussing many of the incidents because it wasn't necessary, and in some instances, for example when discussing problems, disappointments, and disasters, it might have been intrusive.

I also want to thank our public relations director, Jean Zuckerman, our Vice President, Sue Williamson, and my husband for valuable information they gave; Dr. Linda Tway for constructive criticism proofreading the manuscript; Robert Hostage and the editors at Betterway for their continued interest in my work, especially Hilary Swinson for her fine editing. Thanks also to Dr. Robert Secrist and Marilyn King for their advice and to others who contributed in some way to this book, the editors and photographers who kindly gave their permission to reprint their work, and to the staff at Woodmere for their cooperation supplying original prints from their files.

Foreword

When I wrote the Foreword to Pat's first book, *People, Common Sense, and the Small Business*, I was elated to know she was sharing her company's management secrets. Pat and Gene Tway's company was noted for its excellent product and excellent people. Pat told us how others can do what they did to create an ideal work environment that ensures superior performance.

Now in her second book, *Success, Common Sense, and the Small Business*, she shares secrets that ensure success for small business owners — from starting a business to selling it. In her common sense way, she covers everything from personality type and attitude to work habits and fortitude. After reading her book, you will know why people fail or succeed in a small business.

I particularly enjoyed Chapter 5, where Pat talks about the ability of successful people to manage trouble. All of us who own and operate businesses can relate to that, yet most business books avoid discussing disasters. Her willingness to share some of their mistakes, and the mistakes of other successful small business owners, serve as object lessons for anyone in business.

Finally, her analysis of success and how to survive it, in Chapter 6, is one of the best pieces of advice you will get on the subject anywhere. After reading that chapter, you will understand why success spoils some small business owners, and why they either overspend, overwork, or quit work after they succeed.

Anyone who creates a business and sells it worries about whether the business will continue to be successful. The Tways did such an outstanding job during the fourteen years they built their company, Woodmere China, Inc., it would be hard to follow in their footsteps. They supplied china for the King of Saudi Arabia, President Jimmy Carter, and the Vice President's House in Washington, DC, a decorating project I was involved in.

I am proud to say Woodmere, the company they founded and

Pat writes about in her Common Sense books, is still successful. As a member of the President's Inaugural Committee, I was pleased to discover that Woodmere China was selected to design and produce President Bill Clinton's Inaugural Plate. After seeing what Woodmere produced, the selection committee was so pleased it commissioned Woodmere to design and produce a demitasse cup and saucer, and a tea cup and saucer to make a complete dessert set. That's success.

After reading Pat's first two books, *People, Common Sense, and the Small Business* and *Success, Common Sense, and the Small Business*, I am eagerly awaiting her third one.

Carleton Varney
President, Dorothy Draper & Company, Inc.
Dean, Carleton Varney School of Art & Design
University of Charleston

Preface

In *Success, Common Sense, and the Small Business,* Pat Tway has made another valuable addition to the small business literature. Common sense abounds, just as it did in her first book. She is positive and optimistic in her approach to building and maintaining a business. Her emphasis on the customer's needs is standard in marketing literature, but Pat brings this idea to life with examples. She includes the tough examples where they declined business that did not make sense for them or for the customer.

Pat implies that how people manage the business is ultimately more important than the innovative idea behind the business. Many a business built on a competitive and innovative idea fails through lack of attention to the balance of marketing, manufacturing, and financing.

Throughout this book, Pat describes the persistence necessary to build and maintain a successful business. Pat reminds us that trouble is normal. If you view those troubles as "hurdles to leap," like the warehouse fire they experienced, you will manage, learn, and be strengthened.

Pat has lectured at the School of Management at Syracuse University—in the classroom and in our Distinguished Lecture Series. In this book, she displays the same enthusiasm for business and understanding of its challenges that were so obvious in her lectures.

George R. Burman
Dean, Syracuse University School of Management

Contents

Introduction

When I wrote *People, Common Sense, and the Small Business*, I said I would write this book to continue the description of how my husband and I co-founded and co-operated a small business in the ceramic industry. Our marketing company and china decorating plant grew from a home-based venture to a multi-million dollar corporation before we sold it fourteen years later.

My first book describes my end of the business—hiring, training, and managing the people. My husband's end of the business was marketing, selling, and financing the company. This book describes that, from the standpoint of how and why we were successful. Without his end of the business, there would have been no reason for my end of the business. That concept is an important one for small business owners to realize. Without good marketing, selling, and financing, you don't have a business. But you need more to succeed. Everything you do to make your company successful is important, from getting started, goal setting, and promoting your company, to dealing with disasters and surviving success.

Anyone who starts a small business knows that a number of small businesses fail each year. Engineers, plant managers, and cost accountants in our industry, people who started small companies like ours, failed—while our company flourished. Why do some people, like my husband and me, succeed while others fail?

There are many reasons. A major one is the personality type of the owner. That is why the first chapter is devoted to this subject, emphasizing the importance of attitude, selling, and the entrepreneur. You don't become an entrepreneur in school. You only acquire the tools. Gene studied accounting and money management in business college and night classes, but did not earn a degree in business or marketing. I earned a doctoral degree, but it was in anthropology, not business. You become an entrepreneur by doing, and the more you do, the more experience you gain that will help you run your own small business.

Our backgrounds contributed to our success because our work history was varied, from professional musicians to professional salespeople. Gene was a traveling salesman in Kansas working for a New York-based direct sales company while I was working as women's editor for a radio station and training salespeople for Gene. When he was promoted from field sales manager to home office executive, we moved to corporate headquarters in upstate New York. The corporation owned nineteen companies that sold jewelry, cosmetics, nursery stock, and tableware products. Gene worked for the latter company. By the time he was promoted to vice president and board member of the tableware company, he had become a good marketer. In the meantime, I had become a fashion coordinator, copy writer, and jewelry designer for the other companies owned by the same corporation.

While working for the direct sales company, Gene started a mail order catalog for fly-tying materials. Entrepreneurs often start more than one business during a lifetime. Our first one, a mail order business, was also a family enterprise since I helped write the catalog and our daughter and I helped package materials and ship orders. Moonlighting with that small business gave us additional income and business experience, but Gene did not believe it could grow to the size he wanted, so we sold it a few years later.

Gene left the direct selling corporation and joined a china manufacturing company located in Pennsylvania. While he was developing a successful business for them and honing his skills as an entrepreneur, I was conducting doctoral research in industry at the same corporation and studying language and work in a china factory.

With our broad backgrounds, we were ready to start our small china company when the opportunity came. And it came after we had both worked in related industries for over twenty years. When the corporation decided to eliminate the division Gene had developed and promote him to another marketing job with another company the corporation owned, Gene knew it was time to start our own business.

Our company began as a marketing firm selling porcelain products produced for us. We contracted with manufacturers to decorate porcelain dinnerware patterns, which our company sold to distributors in the direct selling field. Within a year, suppliers could not keep pace with our company's sales, so we started our own manufacturing facility. We took a partner to obtain additional capital and bought him out after the first year. We moved our business from our home to a rented building and began decorating porcelain items for the collectibles field, private clubs and restaurants, and a few retail catalogs. The process included importing undecorated porcelain ware, applying decal and gold or platinum lines, firing the ware in kilns and shipping it.

At first I worked part time in the business while teaching at three universities. Later, after the plant manager we hired didn't work out, I joined the company full time and set up the manufacturing operation.

Two years later, we built a 16,000 square foot building. As our business prospered, we rented thousands of feet of additional warehouse space, made frequent business trips to the Orient and Europe, attended trade shows, and took employees on company trips to Hawaii and other places.

Before we sold our business, our china had been selected by the King of Saudi Arabia, a governor, a former President of the United States, and a Vice President. We produced custom china for prestigious clubs, prominent restaurants, and fine retailers, including the Smithsonian catalog and the presidential libraries. All this epitomizes success and exemplifies a good job of marketing.

We drew on our backgrounds and personal experiences and applied common sense to arrive at the techniques that made our company successful. The following pages describe what we did and how we did it. The book also describes what other successful business owners do because I have found a similarity in their attitudes, backgrounds, and sales abilities.

Sharing our experiences and the experiences of other successful business owners will take the mystery out of why some people succeed while others fail. That is why this book cites examples instead of philosophizing about theories.

1.

Establishing a Good Business

One of the most important ways to make certain you have a good business is to have good marketing. For every small business that succeeds, there are several that fail and a few that never get off the ground. In a large majority of cases, the big difference between success and failure is not the product or the service, it's the marketing. Having a great idea, product, or service is not enough. You have to market it.

Sometimes people cannot bring their products to market because of a need for special licenses or government approval. Those potential businesses never come to fruition. We knew someone who invented a self-contained heating element for soups and other canned foods. He showed us how you could heat canned food automatically by pulling a tab from a tiny container of chemicals attached to the bottom of the can. It could have been a great product for campers and travelers, but he did not receive FDA approval and never brought his product to market.

What happened to him happens to a number of people who create new products but can't get government approval before their money runs out. Others create products and obtain patent rights but never successfully market their product. Still others market products they didn't create; some by obtaining the products' patent rights.

That's what happened to a World War II veteran as described by Arthur Godfrey years ago. He stated that a young man was so impressed with a cleaning product he used in the Navy, he sent some to his mother, who used it and asked where she could get more. The young man became so sold on it that after he got out of the service, he researched the product through government offices, obtained the patent rights, and marketed it, creating the Glass Wax Company.

That story illustrates the difference between the successful person who brings a product to market and the creative person who has good ideas but isn't able to market their product. While a few fail because of special licenses they can't obtain, most fail because they do not have the motivation to follow through with a number of factors that ensure success.

MOTIVATION IS IMPORTANT

Many talented people who start small businesses and fail are motivated initially or sporadically but not consistently. They soon burn out, or work in spurts, instead of doing the day-to-day, time-consuming, routine, boring tasks that bring success. Unless the small business owner is *consistently* highly motivated, he or she will not do all the things, day in and day out, that are necessary to succeed.

We were highly motivated. When we started our business, and for the duration of our ownership, we never stopped thinking of new ways to market our product and our company. Other successful business owners we know exhibit the same behavior.

Our business was decorating fine porcelain. We produced custom dinnerware patterns for private clubs and expensive restaurants. We also imported and decorated other porcelain items for the collectibles market. In a broad sense, our competition was any company that did any of those things. In a narrow sense, our competition was only a company that did all of those things. Today there are a number of small china decorating plants like ours. When we started our company, there weren't any exactly like ours.

Gene had a good business idea, and we were both so highly motivated we almost never stopped thinking about it. Consequently, we worked consistently to make it successful. If we were window shopping in a mall, we would stop to admire the porcelain in stores. What we saw would spark an idea for ways to create a new design or to market our product differently.

Often we would talk with the clerk or store manager about their porcelain displays, their suppliers, and the likes and dislikes of their customers. We were so highly motivated by our product and our responsibilities as owners of our company that we never stopped looking for additional ways to market our product, even when we were window shopping for pleasure.

Those qualities that drive the small business owner to work consistently marketing his or her small business are the same qualities that drive a returning veteran to check out a product and obtain patent rights — consistent motivation and follow-through. But those aren't the only qualities that account for success in business.

To have a good business, you need to: (1) have a positive attitude, (2) succeed at selling, and have the attributes of (3) the salesperson, (4) the marketer, and (5) the entrepreneur.

A POSITIVE ATTITUDE

Attitude is the most important determining factor for success in anything. You need a positive attitude to be a successful business owner. Successful people have a positive attitude toward themselves and toward life. Negative people believe success is what makes people have a positive attitude. The reverse is true. A positive attitude is what makes people successful.

Sales manuals and sales trainers offer a number of suggestions for acquiring and maintaining a positive attitude. Gene and I believe so strongly in the concept that it is a part of our personal value system. When we started our company, we made this concept an integral part of our company's stated policies, by requiring a good attitude from every employee, including ourselves.

The Effects of Attitude

Successful people leave their personal problems at home, and never share job-related difficulties with coworkers. Instead, they discuss problems with supervisors who can help. This is a good habit to develop; it can make a big difference in your life.

No matter where you are, or who you are with, if you share problems with others you spread negative attitude. All of us can recall times we have felt good and happy in the morning and by evening have felt down and depressed. The reason is that people have either shared their negative thoughts with us or reacted in a negative way toward us. The result is we feel negative too.

If you have a negative attitude, you attract negative things. If you have a positive attitude, you attract positive things, including positive people and positive situations. Psychologists describe the effects of what we think about and expect to happen as *self-fulfilling prophecy*. This is a good way of saying you create your own destiny by your attitude toward yourself and toward life.

Attitude and Fear

Fear prevents many people from having a positive attitude. People may be afraid of: criticism, competition, ridicule, loss of respect, loss of love, failure, poverty, illness, and death. In the depths of the Depression, Franklin Roosevelt reminded the nation that all we had to fear was fear itself. Fear incapacitates us by limiting our abilities to think and act rationally.

There is a story about a traveler who met the Plague on the

edge of a great city and asked, "Where are you going?" The Plague answered, "To the city to slay 5,000 people." Later, the traveler met the Plague and said, "You told me you were going to kill 5,000, but I heard 50,000 died." The Plague replied, "I did kill only 5,000. The others were killed by Fear."

You must conquer fear before you can succeed. That means you must guard against doubt, which is another manifestation of fear. You can do this by replacing doubts and fears with positive thoughts. If a doubtful thought enters your mind, stop it and replace it with a positive thought. If you find yourself worrying about poverty, replace that fear and worry with positive images of success and abundance.

Successful people operate on the premise that a positive attitude brings positive results. A continued positive approach brings a positive destiny. Champion athletes say they try to think positive thoughts about their game before they play it. A trainer of champion bird dogs, who spends long hours teaching dogs, told us he visualizes each dog perfectly performing the maneuvers of the field trial before the trial begins. He does this before every field trial and considers this mental exercise — planting a positive attitude in himself and the dog — an important ingredient of his success.

Perhaps it is the way we approach something when we have a positive attitude toward it that makes us successful. Whatever the reason, I know that it works because I have seen it work. This technique has worked for me and it has worked for Gene. It is something good salespeople, marketers, entrepreneurs, and small business owners practice consistently.

Attitude and Health

Even the medical profession has recognized the need for people to have a positive attitude for better health and to increase longevity. Norman Cousins spent the last years of his life traveling to medical symposiums convincing that profession of the importance of positive and happy thoughts for patient recovery.

Magazines and newspapers carry articles by physicians, psychologists, psychotherapists, and psychiatrists urging people to adopt a positive attitude. Dr. Bernie Siegel writes books demonstrating the healing power of a positive attitude. He and other authors list a number of activities that can help people develop the habit of maintaining a positive attitude. Some of the suggestions I have encountered over the years are discussed below.

One is the notion that when we talk to ourselves we are feeding our subconscious mind information that will bring about results. A common analogy used for our subconscious mind is that of the computer. It does what it is programmed to do without rationalizing. If we feed it positive information, we get positive results. If we feed it negative information, we get negative results.

Psychologists have conducted experiments to show that your subconscious mind believes what you tell it. When people were told to close their eyes and imagine they were standing on the ledge of a high building, their pulse rates increased. Some people even felt queasy.

How many times have you had the experience of reacting physically to something you thought occurred, only to learn later that it never happened? You body responded as if the situation you only imagined had actually transpired.

Acquiring a Good Attitude

We are reminded that everything in the physical world existed first in the mental world, as a thought or an idea. Thomas Edison's electric light bulb was first a thought, a mental image. Most anything you do, you think about first and create in your mind. Thoughts can and do manifest themselves in the physical world.

Another analogy that has been used to demonstrate the power of thought is that a thought is like a seed. If we plant a seed in the earth and give it water, it sprouts and eventually breaks above ground where we can see what it has produced. If we have a thought, we plant it in our subconscious mind. By recalling it, we water it so that it grows and eventually manifests itself in the physical world.

Your subconscious mind can work for you if you use it in a positive way. Experts also suggest that when you catch yourself having negative thoughts, you should replace them with positive ones. However, they warn not to replace a negative thought with a positive thought that includes a negative expression. For example, when you think, "I'm a failure," don't replace it with, "I'm not a failure." Instead, substitute it with a positive way of expressing the thought—"I'm a success"—while visualizing yourself in a successful situation.

Try to visualize positive results for projects in your business. Visualize each important encounter that will affect your business and picture the outcome as positive. Try to create the actual picture of whom you will see, what you will say, and how they will react. You need not be specific with every detail. You want to visualize a general impression of positive results. We know many successful people who often do this before an important encounter at the bank, a major sales presentation, or a decisive business conference.

Every time you think of your business, even when things look gloomiest, visualize your business in a positive way. It may appear unrealistic to do this, but I urge you to do it *because it works.* We believe so strongly in the power of a positive attitude that I attached the following messages to all our telephones at work:

OUR WORK BRINGS SUCCESS, ABUNDANCE, AND HARMONY.
OUR WORKERS ARE HAPPY, HARMONIOUS, AND PRODUCTIVE.

Devise your own method for establishing the habit of positive thinking because what you think about expands into reality. One final warning researchers give is to stay away from negative thinkers. If you must be with them, make a point of changing the subject anytime the conversation becomes negative. You need to have a positive attitude to be a successful business owner. You also need to sell.

SUCCEED AT SELLING

To succeed in business, you need to succeed at selling. People who want something need to present their desires in the best possible light to get what they want, whether it's money or cooperation.

The dictionary definition for *selling* includes, "to develop a belief in the truth, value, or desirability of ... to persuade or influence to a course of action or to the acceptance of something ... to cause or promote ...." The dictionary definition of *profession* includes, "a principal calling, vocation, or employment ... the whole body of persons engaged in a calling." Those descriptions combined define the selling profession.

Everyone Sells

Whether people engage in the selling profession full time or borrow techniques from it to get what they want, they succeed to the degree that they use selling skills. Stockbrokers, attorneys, contractors, accountants, and many others rely on good selling techniques to get what they want, when they want it. If they don't know how to sell their ideas, needs, or wants to those who can satisfy them, they don't succeed.

The physician who persuades the hospital board to provide more equipment is selling. The hospital administrator who convinces the community to contribute more funds for another hospital wing is selling. The diplomat who counsels world leaders to act cautiously is selling. The committee chair who convinces others to follow a certain course of action is selling.

Grant proposals, contract bids, and business plans are all sales presentations of one kind or another. Based on dictionary definitions, the motives and actions of successful people from every profession are those of people who sell. Selling is necessary for success in any field, especially for the small business.

I think selling should be a required course in school. It should include field work too. Students could earn money while learning. You can't learn to sell by talking about it. You need to *do* it. Such classes would also put selling in proper perspective and benefit everyone, especially the students.

Types of Selling

If you have not had sales training, I suggest you get some now. You will gain the most valuable experience selling for companies that market their product directly to the consumer than from companies that sell through retail outlets. Sales companies usually give better training because they must rely on selling skills to generate interest in their products. Retail outlets give less training, and as a result the salesperson in most cases merely takes orders.

We were lucky to have been associated with a good sales company for many years, and they trained us thoroughly. What we learned from that company contributed to our success in everything we did. The basic characteristics and good habits you develop from working with a top flight sales organization can help you succeed in whatever career you choose.

There are several kinds of sales companies. We worked for direct sales companies. Those companies sell direct to the consumer in his or her home, either door to door without an invitation, or by appointment as a result of a referral from someone else, who may or may not own the product. They may sell to individuals or to several people at a home party.

Cosmetics, jewelry, clothing, kitchen utensils, and a number of other products are marketed by direct sales companies. The companies we worked for sold nursery stock, cosmetics, jewelry, and tableware products such as flatware, china, and crystal.

My husband worked for the company that sold tableware products. He was promoted from salesman to field manager, sales manager, vice president, and finally was elected to their board of directors. My mother worked as a salesperson and field manager for the same company. I sold for them and later wrote sales promotion for some of their companies. I designed jewelry for their manufacturing firm and was a fashion coordinator for one of their jewelry sales companies.

During those years we gained great respect for salespeople, which offset the negative impression so often associated with that occupation. For years I heard people denigrate the selling profession with comments about "the used car salesman" as personifying the lowest form of worker.

Contrasted with this, I have heard my husband repeatedly say with pride, "I'm a salesman," when people compliment him on his marketing skills. He recognizes that good marketing is really good selling. Narrowly defined by large corporations, marketing entails specific duties in a limited sphere of activity. Broadly defined by small business owners, marketing entails everything you do to make your business successful. Gene knows that without selling there would be no marketing. He is a good salesman and proud of it. Most successful marketers, entrepreneurs, and small business owners are. They personify the best qualities of the salesperson.

THE SALESPERSON

A Winning Personality

There are a number of attributes that characterize a good salesperson. The one most often associated with salespeople is enthusiasm. Good salespeople are enthusiastic about themselves, their products, and their companies. They can project enthusiasm about whatever they are doing. They are somewhat like actors who, even though they may feel slightly depressed or ill, project an image of alertness, brightness, and interest in what they are doing. They exhibit enthusiasm.

Gene is a good example of an enthusiastic salesperson. Even when he didn't feel well, or was tired from a long business trip, he was always able to convey enthusiasm to our customers, our vendors, and our employees. He knew if you project enthusiasm for what you are doing, others are soon emulating you because enthusiasm is contagious. When you are enthused, you create an atmosphere that is conducive to positive results, you enjoy life more, and people enjoy being with you more. You also generate more sales.

Another quality salespeople have is optimism. This is why having a positive attitude is so important. Optimism is the result of a positive attitude, which I described in an earlier section. I heard a sales trainer once say, "Optimism is the true Philosopher's Stone, which turns to gold everything it touches." She also told us that, "A pessimist finds difficulty in every opportunity, while an optimist finds opportunity in every difficulty." She illustrated the point by telling about two shoe salesmen who were given new territories in a primitive country. One salesman wired home, "We can't sell shoes here. No one is wearing any." The other salesman wired, "Ship another boatload. We can really sell shoes here. No one has any."

While writing sales promotion I witnessed several situations like the one just described. When a sales contest was underway some salespeople would be selling very little and complaining about their bad territory. Other salespeople working in the same territory would be making outstanding sales records. The good salespeople were optimistic and believed they had a great territory. A good salesperson we know maintains, "It's not the bum territory. It's the bum in the territory" that makes the difference.

Salespeople generally have a strong belief system. They believe strongly in themselves, their products, and their companies. They also believe in the law of averages, and work consistently with that notion. I still remember Gene and me flipping a coin repeatedly to prove that 50% of the time it will come up heads if you flip it enough times. One of the first things good salespeople do as they improve their selling skills is to discover what the law of averages is for sales of their products.

Salespeople know you have to make enough presentations of your product for the law of averages to work. They also realize you never know which presentation will result in a sale. Therefore, they make every presentation enthusiastically and optimistically with the belief that they will close a sale, which leads to their next quality.

Following Through to Meet Goals

Good salespeople always follow through and try to close the order. People who make presentations of their product and never try to close their sales are like people who write books and never send them to publishers. Learning to close an order is either a talent good salespeople have or a skill they develop. The companies we worked for had thorough training programs that taught people how to close orders.

I remember a series of buying signals they described. When the customer was attentive, asked questions, handled the product, talked possessively about it, asked about the cost or the payment schedule, voiced concerns, or asked about deliveries, the customer was exhibiting buying signals. If salespeople ignore these buying signals without answering questions or focusing the buyer's attention on taking action, they are missing sales.

Salespeople are goal oriented. They learn early in their careers the importance of setting and striving to meet goals. In Marilyn vos Savant's column, someone asked if it is best for a person to strive to achieve a goal without the gifts necessary to achieve it, or to face reality and work with what one has. She answered,

"Goals, I believe, do far more for our character and for our world than gifts have ever done. So, go for your dreams, dear reader, and let me know what happens." (*Parade*, 5/24/92, p. 29)

Striving to meet goals is the difference between really successful people and moderately successful people. Gene and I set goals for everything we did, from the moment we decided to start our company to the day we sold it fourteen years later. We believe so strongly in the part goal-setting played in our success that I devote an entire chapter to it later in this book.

Setting goals is closely associated with another quality salespeople have — self determination. They believe they have the power to control what happens to them. They believe the harder they work, the more successful they will be. They do not look for excuses when things go wrong, or rely on others to do their work. People with self determination put forth more effort because they truly believe they control their own destinies. They don't wait for someone to hand them success; they know they have to work for it.

Friendly and Adaptable

Networking is another quality of salespeople. I have heard more than one successful salesperson say, "Good selling is really building bridges and establishing networks." Some people mistake this for making personal friends. To be a good salesperson you need to be friendly but you need to recognize the difference between making friends and establishing friendly contacts to discuss business. Most personal friends, like families, don't buy from you. Friendly business contacts do, or they lead you to others who do.

Salespeople are adaptable. They have the ability to fit in and be comfortable with others while making others feel comfortable with them. They know that people buy when they are comfortable. They also know that they sell best when they are comfortable too. If they are intimidated by their clients or their clients' surroundings, they don't do as well.

You must fit your customer and your company to do your best. As a salesperson, the company you work for automatically defines your market and your customers. That means you need to dress and behave to fit those markets and those customers. In anthropology this adaptive behavior is referred to as *borrowing status*. Here are some examples.

If you visit a Rolls-Royce showroom, the salesperson you meet there will be different in appearance and demeanor from the one you meet at a Chevy truck showroom. The salesperson at a Gucci store does not exhibit the same behavior pattern, language, or dress as the salesperson at a K-Mart. Are salespeople better because of where they work or what they sell? Not always. Some of the best salespeople I have encountered worked at discount stores, and some of the worst work at exclusive showrooms.

What makes the difference? The ability of the salesperson to make the customer feel comfortable. Whether the selling venue is an exclusive boutique or an open warehouse, customers respond best to good salespeople who conform to their surroundings and accommodate the clientele.

In our small company, we always dressed conservatively because of the clientele to whom we were selling. While we were friendly, we were never overly casual. For example, we never sat on desks, put our feet on furniture, or walked into someone's office aggressively without being invited.

We always traveled in business suits because we wanted to be sure we were dressed appropriately in case our luggage was lost. Many business people carry their luggage on airlines to avoid losing it. We always carried our briefcases on airlines so we could work while traveling and to avoid the possibility of losing them.

Customer Oriented

Salespeople are customer oriented. They want to help the customer. They ask questions and make recommendations. They may even send customers to competitors, or they may suggest buying fewer items if they feel it is in the customer's best interests. Their concern for their customers leads naturally to repeat business and word-of-mouth advertising. Here's an example of that quality applied in a small business.

Gene was always concerned about the customer and took care not to sell more than he thought the customer could afford. I am sure one reason was his desire to avoid creating customers who would become collection problems. More important than that, however, he was concerned that if he oversold a client it would hurt that client.

When one marketer of collector plates asked us to produce an artist's work on collector plates to be sold in gift shops, the customer indicated he wanted to produce 10,000 plates. When he asked Gene how many plates he should produce initially, Gene suggested he start with a far smaller quantity. Gene worried that the customer would not sell as many as he thought he could and would suffer cash flow problems. The customer took Gene's advice. However, the plate was a big success, which no one could have predicted, and the customer had to order another complete set of decals to produce more plates in a hurry before we had completed his first order.

Although in this case Gene's concern for the customer caused the customer some hectic days waiting for the second shipment to fill orders, he appreciated Gene's concern for him and his potential cash flow problems. Gene's concern for the customer got us a series of sales from this person over the next few years. This customer also recommended us to other people who were looking for a manufacturer they could trust.

Small business owners need to remember this example when they are tempted to sell a customer more than the customer needs, even if the customer suggests it. Your business will be more successful in the long run if you always try to do the right thing for your customers, even if at first it seems not to have a direct benefit to your business.

Listening is Selling

A salesperson does not talk people into buying. People like to buy and want to buy. A good salesperson listens to customers and helps them focus on what to buy and when to buy, to satisfy their needs and make them feel good. Salespeople have a saying that exemplifies this. "If you want to know why John Doe buys then look at things through John Doe's eyes."

One of the major reasons Gene started our business was because he listened to the customers and saw a need in our industry to give the customer what the customer wanted, not what the manufacturer had to sell. The majority of our business was decorating fine porcelain to the customers' specifications.

Top salesman Zig Ziglar reminds us that "talking is sharing, listening is caring." You need to listen to know what the customer wants or doesn't want. A salesperson is a good listener as well as a good talker. Many times salespeople are so eager to tell their story they don't listen to the customer. By listening they might learn the customer is already sold and wants to ask about another of the company's products. When salespeople don't listen, they run the risk of losing the sale.

There is a story that sales trainers tell to impress upon salespeople the dangers of talking too much. "Samson killed 10,000 Philistines with the jawbone of an ass. Every day 10,000 sales are killed with the same weapon."

A salesperson handles complaints willingly and politely. Nothing is 100% perfect. Everyone makes mistakes; even the best companies with the highest quality products slip sometimes. A salesperson listens first, then takes steps to improve the situation or to replace the product. That leads to another good quality, going the extra mile.

Going the Extra Mile

A salesperson is willing to go the extra mile for the customer and the company. That is a major difference between an order taker and a salesperson. Anyone can take an order. A salesperson goes the extra mile to make certain the customer is satisfied. That may mean checking with the customer after the sale has been made or checking at the time of delivery. Going the extra mile pays great dividends.

We knew a direct sales nursery stock company that failed, partly because no one checked back with the customer when the product was delivered. I devised the method for selling their products using colorful catalogs that salespeople presented at home parties. The company had a high success rate selling orders but also had a high cancellation rate for orders.

The customers visualized what they ordered as beautiful, colorful flowers and shrubs. What they saw delivered were small dormant plants and bulbs. No salesperson dropped by to remind the customer how beautiful the plants would be in a short while. No one realized only half the sale was made at the party. The other half had to be made at the time of delivery. The company would probably still be in business today if salespeople had gone the extra mile for the customer.

Persistence Pays Off

Another important quality salespeople have is persistence. They continue working even when they are not highly motivated. Despite the boring parts of a project or the difficulties encountered, they don't give up easily. Many times Gene has doggedly continued working on a problem long after others would have quit. Working resolutely and persistently can make the difference between solving a problem and not solving it.

Being persistent means working consistently — not sporadically. Many people have sporadic work habits that prevent them from being successful. The successful salesperson is a hard worker, not just some of the time but all of the time. Working consistently to win the race has been taught to most of us since childhood with the story of the tortoise and the hare.

I can still picture the preschool reader that showed the fast-running hare darting through the pages, playing tennis and wasting time all sorts of ways, while the slow-moving tortoise kept plodding along. And I can remember the frustration on the last page when the hare missed the finish line by a nose.

To have a good business, you need to have the attributes of a salesperson. You also need to have the qualities of a marketer.

THE MARKETER

Planning for the Competitive Edge

A marketer is a good salesperson, but a good salesperson is not necessarily a good marketer. Marketers have other qualities that many salespeople do not have. One of the major ones is the ability to plan ahead, not only for themselves but for others. They can conceptualize where the market is going and how their company can take advantage of that direction. They can devise a strategy that utilizes the skills of many people to achieve their goals for the company.

Marketers have the ability to examine the market, searching for niches where the company has a competitive edge. They are concerned not only with sales but with gross margins and with operating expenses they control, such as advertising, product development, travel, and entertainment. Their plans must include the right product, the right market, and the right timing with the right profit margins if they are to achieve the company's goals.

To be a good marketer, you need to plan your company's position in a particular market and set sales goals for the next few years. Your goals must outline what to expect. You cannot operate with "pie in the sky" notions. Your plans must be realistic and achievable, so they can be used by the production manager to schedule manufacturing, by the sales manager to arrange the sales force's activities, and by the financial manager to plan for cash flow.

Defining the Company's Market

Another quality the marketer has is the ability to define the company's universe accurately. That means being able to identify how much of the industry's total market the company can penetrate. The marketer's job is to know if the time is right, what type of product is best, whether the product fits the company's manufacturing capabilities, its distribution network, and its image, and whether the company can afford the project.

When Gene was director of marketing for the commercial division of the large china company, he wrote a marketing plan in which he defined the universe for the commercial division. He applied those same techniques when defining the universe for our small business. Below is a sheet depicting a portion of his early marketing plan for our small company.

Conducting Research

Conducting and managing research projects is another talent of the marketer. Marketers recognize the importance of the customer profile and design programs to examine it. They have a

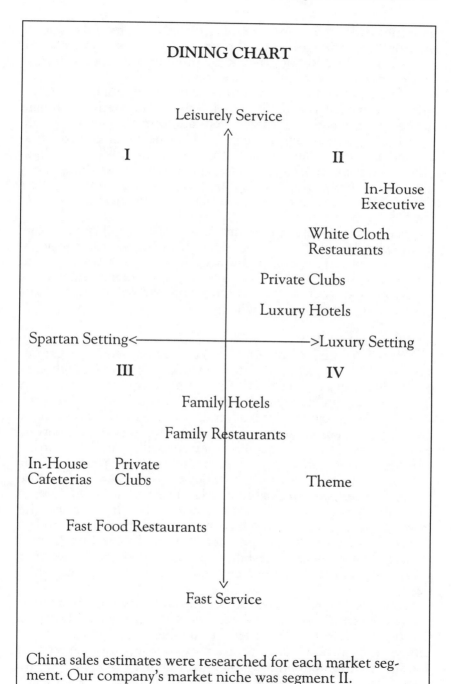

DINING CHART

China sales estimates were researched for each market segment. Our company's market niche was segment II.

wide network of business contacts to draw on for information, and they know how to utilize the reports of others to process that information. In addition, they know how to use reports from libraries, trade associations, and the government.

Marketers know how to utilize advertising, public relations, special promotions, trade shows, distribution networks, merchandising, and the activities of sales reps and other company personnel to achieve their marketing goals. They help plan the advertising and promotion campaigns for their companies. While they may draw on outside sources to do the majority of these things, they have the ability to think ahead, to create, and to draw together the activities of a number of people to bring their products to market successfully.

Another characteristic of marketers is the ability to isolate and explore problems affecting sales. They are aware of regional and seasonal differences in the market and know when to use short-term tactics, such as sales discounts, to address immediate problems, and when to rely on long-range strategies, such as advertising, to satisfy larger challenges.

Developing Products

Marketers are keenly aware of the need for good product development. They have the ability to work with artists and designers or engineers to create or improve company products. Many marketers are highly creative people who can help design products or create programs for launching products. They know every product has a particular life span, and trying to extend it beyond its time is useless. Consequently, they are willing and eager to try new ideas, new products, and new ways to sell new products.

One of the most destructive things a company can do is refuse to admit when a product's life is over. The marketing division of the china company Gene worked for was influenced by the manufacturing division, which persisted in producing the product easiest for the company to produce. No one listened to the customers. The company's inability to satisfy their customers was what eventually drove their customers overseas to satisfy their needs.

As a marketer, you need to be constantly alert to the changing needs of the customer. When you sense his needs changing, you need to respond. Don't let the supplier or manufacturer dictate what you should sell. Your ability to assess the market puts you in a position of control. You need to tell the supplier and the manufacturer what you want them to produce to satisfy the needs of the customers.

Good Timing and Market Trends

The marketer has good timing and can spot trends. A bell curve is used to illustrate the life of a product. At the peak of the bell anyone can tell you a product is selling well. A good salesperson can tell you which products have sold well and which are currently selling well. A marketer can tell you which products will sell well in the future. They have a good eye for their markets and their industries.

To be a good marketer, you need to recognize the importance of reaching the market ahead of your company's competitors. The marketer's goal is to be on the leading edge and set trends, not just follow them. A good example of this is the trend for black dinnerware patterns Gene introduced into the tableware market in the early 1960s. Before that time black was considered a bad color for dinnerware. No one was selling black. Gene had an intuitive hunch that black would become important in the tableware industry. As director of marketing for a large china manufacturer, he developed a marketing strategy that included introducing black dinnerware and black crystal into the direct sales market. It was an instant hit, and soon other manufacturers were following this trend.

Knowledge of the Market

How did Gene know black would be good? He was closely associated with a number of retail and commercial outlets in the tableware industry. He was constantly looking at magazines in the restaurant and tableware fields. In addition, he was aware of the amount of black being used in architectural design, home furnishings, and in the fashion and jewelry industry. While he does not remember consciously studying those things, he noticed them subconsciously and they had an effect on him.

If you are keenly aware of your market, following the trade papers and other media sources that relate in some way to your field, you can often sense what is coming next. Here is another example.

At one time I was designing jewelry, and immersed in the fashion industry, studying all the trade papers relating to clothing and jewelry. I designed a gold pin in the shape of an open pea pod that held six pearls. It was a good design and very timely. The day after I designed it, I saw the identical pin on the cover of a leading jewelry trade paper.

How could it have happened? The other artists in the studio told me that whatever I'm thinking of, others who have access to the same cultural data are thinking of at the same time. That is why more than one person invented the telephone at the same time and why different people create similar products simultaneously.

Flexibility for a Changing Market

Good marketers are flexible yet consistent. They don't ignore the road map they have set for themselves and others, but when necessary they are willing to consider alternate routes to reach their goals. They are perceptive enough to watch the market, know when it is changing, and rearrange segments of their plans to take advantage of the changing market.

Good marketers, like good salespeople, have qualities that lay the foundation for the success of a small business, but the ultimate traits necessary to ensure success are possessed by entrepreneurs.

THE ENTREPRENEUR

Every successful small business owner we know is an entrepreneur. I have pointed out additional abilities marketers have that salespeople don't necessarily have. There are also additional abilities entrepreneurs have that marketers don't necessarily have. You need all these qualities if you are going to succeed as a small business owner. In other words, you need to be a salesperson, a marketer, *and* an entrepreneur.

We have known a number of excellent salespeople and marketers who have tried to start their own companies and failed. Why can't good marketers automatically succeed as business owners? That puzzled us until we enumerated additional qualities successful business owners share that some good salespeople and good marketers do not. These are the qualities of an entrepreneur.

The Effects of Home

Profiles of entrepreneurs describe them as the eldest child in a family; a person whose parents owned a business at one time; one who perceives obstacles as problems to solve; one who takes calculated risks, sets high standards, and prefers self employment. Whether every entrepreneur fits that profile I can't say. The entrepreneurs we know generally fit that description.

Qualities that identify an entrepreneur may come naturally to some people, or they may be acquired over the years through experience or through early contact with entrepreneurs. If a person grows up in a family that has owned its own business, even briefly, that person has an advantage over the person who has not learned about business while growing up. He or she learns the total dedication, long hours, and family participation required of small business owners. That person learns there are no permanent solutions to problems and no guarantees of success. Enculturation is important; we learn from our home environment.

Some entrepreneurs start several different businesses. Their interests and energies are focused on starting businesses, not running them beyond a certain size. They operate them successfully for short periods, become bored, and sell them. Other entrepreneurs start a business and keep it for a number of years, or perhaps for their lifetime.

Concern for Supplies and Cash Flow

One of the qualities entrepreneurs share is the ability to look ahead. To look ahead doesn't mean only thinking in terms of sales and commissions, but in terms of a number of things that contribute to total success. The entrepreneur has the habit of translating every sale or contact into future sales and, beyond that, into what those sales mean to the company in terms of profits and in terms of liabilities that may be incurred by the sale. This is an important difference between a marketer and an entrepreneur. The entrepreneur is constantly concerned with those things.

The entrepreneur also thinks in terms of how much gross margin it will take to generate the cash to cover current operating expenses of the company and what will be needed in addition as a result of sales. The entrepreneur knows that if sales aren't made today, there will be no income next month or next year.

The entrepreneur, unlike most marketers, is very concerned with having the correct amount of product to keep as inventory to fulfill orders, and how much it costs to keep that inventory. He doesn't want too much or too little. If the company also manufactures the products, the entrepreneur projects how much inventory must be kept of components needed to produce the product and the lead time for ordering those components.

Gene was always concerned with each of the components of inventory, down to shipping cartons, mailing labels, and packing supplies. He knew you must have alternate sources for obtaining supplies if an emergency prevents your regular suppliers from meeting their deadlines.

You have to be concerned with projected sales, projected cash flow, and projected labor requirements to produce and ship your product and service your customers. Although separate managers may be handling some of these specific duties, the owner has to be concerned about them and make projections based on the knowledge he or she has about the company's needs. Projecting as a habit is a necessary attribute of the small business owner. Without it, the business will not succeed for long.

Timely Decisions are Critical

The entrepreneur is good at making rapid decisions. People who have trouble making decisions will never succeed as small business owners because decisions have to be made daily. Some of them may be more urgent than others but all of them are important from the standpoint of good timing. People who can't make timely decisions are detrimental to any business, and especially destructive to the small business. Here is an example.

We are acquainted with a small business owner who sold his company to a large corporation and recommended a person as a good replacement for himself. The large corporation's personnel manager, who was in charge of searching for the owner's replacement, was so fearful of making a decision he postponed it for six months and the applicant took another similar job.

The personnel manager waited another six months in a state of indecision until the corporation was forced to hire someone in haste. As a result, they hired the wrong man and had to replace him after a year. The personnel director's lack of decisive action cost the large corporation and the small business they had just acquired hundreds of thousands of dollars.

Every decision a small business owner makes is important in one way or another. Entrepreneurs know they have to make decisions. They recognize that the only bad decision is no decision. When you make decisions, you take control of situations. When you postpone decisions, you forfeit control.

At our daughter's doctoral graduation, the dean giving the commencement address said there are three kinds of people in the world: those who make things happen, those who watch things happen, and those who say, "What happened?" Entrepreneurs make things happen and may watch things happen, but they seldom ask, "What happened?"

Solving Problems Ensures Success

Entrepreneurs enjoy solving problems and putting together "deals." When they encounter a problem in their business, they do not entertain the thought of failure. They look at the problem as something to solve—not something to defeat them. They view negative situations as challenges rather than unsolvable problems. When they encounter misfortune or adversity, they work even harder, because they perceive what happened to them as a temporary setback—not a failure. (This is discussed in more detail in the chapter dealing with trouble.)

Entrepreneurs learn from every experience. They may not keep journals or outline workbooks about their experiences; their basic temperament often precludes this. However, they reap the best from their experiences and never let the worst dampen their enthusiasm for the next project, which is always just around the corner.

That special optimistic quality is balanced with other qualities that protect them from becoming unrealistic dreamers. Dreamers never quite make it, or, if they do, let it slip through their fingers time and again. When entrepreneurs find the right project, they develop it to its fullest. They modestly call it luck. Others call it talent, even genius.

Whatever the underlying reason, entrepreneurs constantly aim toward success and do not dwell on failure. If they make mistakes, they are the first to admit it, learn from it, and move on. We heard one entrepreneur say, "The fact that you've shot yourself in the foot is not as important as how fast you can reload."

There were times while we owned our business that I wondered how Gene could continue working on a problem when it appeared there wasn't a solution. He would persist, exploring different avenues until he found a solution. Here is an example.

We started the manufacturing end of our business because Gene's suppliers could not keep pace with orders from our marketing company. At the time we started our decorating facility we had no building, no equipment, and not enough money for either. There were orders waiting to be produced and seemingly no way to produce them. Within a short time, Gene had found a way to surmount these obstacles and we were on our way. (I will discuss how he did it in more detail in the next chapter.) The point I want to emphasize here is, he was determined not to let anything become a reason for failure.

Taking Calculated Risks

Doing what Gene did was risky, but entrepreneurs take risks when they see opportunities to get ahead. They do not take long shots with the odds weighted heavily against them, but they do take calculated risks. Unless a person is willing to take risks, he or she will probably not succeed in business. The small business owner is continually taking calculated risks. Just being in business is a calculated risk.

I was with Gene when a customer asked if we could supply a certain item. I almost answered no. However, I kept silent because I knew never to interfere when a salesperson is working.

To my surprise Gene said, "Yes, I think we can get that for you."

After we left, I asked Gene how he could say yes when we both knew we had no way of supplying that item. Gene quickly said we didn't know for sure that we couldn't supply it. We only thought that way now. If we did some checking we might discover some way to have it produced for us and then we could supply it. He was right, of course, and we got the order. What appeared as an insurmountable obstacle to me was simply a "thorny business problem" for him. I knew then being in business was no place for people who were quick to say no, or who were not willing to take calculated risks.

Opportunity is Everywhere

This example of taking a risk for an opportunity demonstrates another quality entrepreneurs share. They are opportunistic. They perceive most situations as ways to get ahead, make a deal, or establish a network for some future business. Entrepreneurs are constantly looking for new ways to expand their market, target their distribution, improve their product, locate a new supplier, or help a customer. They see opportunities beyond those that good salespeople or marketers see. They see opportunity everywhere. Here is another example.

At one time I was sending promotion letters to associations that were due to celebrate anniversaries. We obtained a number of orders for commemorative plates through this procedure. One potential customer called and mentioned his company also produced a catalog for employees. I felt he might be interested in something more than a single commemorative plate, so I turned the call over to Gene.

Gene sold the customer much more than a commemorative plate for one occasion. He sold a series of collector plates for eight years. What I saw as a $10,000 order—selling a commemorative plate and an additional item for the catalog—Gene saw as an opportunity to sell more than $100,000 in plates yearly for the next eight years.

When I asked him what made him think of it, he answered that he really didn't think of it in terms of dollars. He saw an opportunity to help the customer solve a problem. As he visited with the man and asked him about his business, the man told Gene he had a problem every year finding items for his catalog. Gene told him about the advantages of using a series of collector plates to depict interesting stories. The customer became so excited he decided to order a series of collector plates depicting historical scenes of his company. The scenes came from old pictures his company owned. Gene found an artist to style them so they could be produced as decal that we could decorate on porcelain plates.

Although entrepreneurs take risks when they see opportunities, they will not risk their money by throwing it away on projects they know nothing about or have not researched. They manage money wisely; not always conservatively, but wisely. There is a difference. They worry about money but they realize that you need to spend money to make money. They will invest in new projects, promotion materials, new equipment, and travel when it helps the business.

Attention to Detail

Entrepreneurs are aggressive learners and have an insatiable curiosity, not necessarily about everything but about things that interest them at a particular time. When they are interested in a subject, they pursue it from every angle. They often become amateur experts in their hobbies. Gene has an extensive flyfishing library, has tied fishing flies for fifty years, and has taken fly-casting lessons intermittently for over twenty years.

Entrepreneurs tend to want to do it all themselves rather than rely on others to provide information for them. This leads to another important quality: the need to check every detail. No detail is too small or job too unimportant for them to check out or to do. They are not status conscious and therefore will attend to small details themselves. I'm reminded of a story Gene told when he returned from a management training course many years ago.

The instructor was denigrating a corporate officer for taking his time to check with a local manager that the electricity had been turned off when his company moved. Gene said the class sniggered with the teacher, while Gene thought the corporate manager had done the proper thing. He was thinking like a business owner. Gene always remembered the incident and how wrong everyone's thinking was.

Two incidents in particular exemplify for me the entrepreneur's attention to detail. The first is seeing Carleton Varney, columnist and President of Dorothy Draper Ltd., New York, sweeping the front sidewalk of his newest Sarasota store to "help out" on opening day. The second was seeing my hair stylist personally setting the tiny trees in front of his salon on opening day.

Their personal attention to details is partly the result of being worriers. While these entrepreneurs are not negative people, they are perceptive and see potential disaster looming ahead and try to avoid it. They feel they have the power to control what happens to them as long as they are prepared. That is why they watch for potential problems so they can be prepared. They keep a sharp eye—and they worry.

Working with Urgency Requires Energy

This leads to another quality entrepreneurs have that a few good salespeople and marketers have, but not to the same degree. Entrepreneurs work with a sense of urgency. Everything they do has to be done now, not later. They are the antithesis of the procrastinator. They are so driven to succeed, they never postpone anything, even if it means working twelve, fourteen, and sometimes eighteen hours a day, every day.

Entrepreneurs have good health and boundless energy, therefore they set a heady pace. For the duration Gene and I worked in our business, we worked from early morning till evening. Gene always took work home on evenings and weekends. He often came back in the evenings to check on something. When we traveled, we worked the same schedule and came directly to the office from the airport, no matter how long our trip had been. When someone remarked on this to Gene, he replied, "We have important messages and mail that need to be checked now, not later."

We especially appreciated working with the Japanese because, unlike American and European industries that operate on short work weeks, the Japanese work the same hours as small business owners do in the United States. It is costly to travel overseas so we liked being able to work long hours and weekends on our Japanese business trips. We often worked Sundays with our Japanese business contacts, and they were eager to do so. Their work ethic was refreshing and certainly saved us money since we could conduct a great deal of business in a limited amount of time.

The qualities I have described are the major ones I have observed in Gene and other successful entrepreneurs. The degree to which small business owners exemplify these characteristics is the degree to which you can measure their success. If you share these attributes, you have the basic qualifications to be a small business owner. If you do not have them, you should work to acquire them.

2.

Getting Started

There are three ways to get started in a small business: you can inherit it, you can buy it, or you can create it yourself. No matter how you acquire your business, your success or failure depends on *you*. To succeed, small business owners must have keen marketing skills, be acquainted with their industry, and have financial insight. They may have more skill in one area than another, but they need some skill in all three to succeed.

Whatever attributes business owners lack, they must rely on others to supply. Gene was strong in marketing and finances but lacked manufacturing and personnel experience. Therefore, when we added the decorating plant, he relied on me to run it. My doctoral dissertation was based on industrial research at a china factory and encompassed production techniques and scheduling. Since work in anthropology includes human relations, he also relied on me to hire, train, and manage the people for both companies. He didn't want to be bothered with that end of the business. Most entrepreneurs don't. If you don't, be sure you hire someone who does.

Inheriting a Business

If you inherit your small business, you also inherit the way the business is run, whether it's good or bad. You inherit what people expect of you and the business. Those expectations also include how others think you should run the business. Even though you inherit a business, you still must assert yourself and run it with the same expertise as any successful business owner.

I have known small business owners who failed after inheriting sizeable fortunes along with their small businesses. As I look back on these people, I know they did not have the abilities necessary to run a business, even though it was running successfully at the time they inherited it. They would have been luckier had they inherited the *attributes* needed to run a business rather than the business itself.

We have also known successful business owners who inherited small businesses and built them into sizable fortunes. We have a friend who inherited an electrical company and a construction company from his father. He worked in the business all his life, doing chores after school and on weekends. He attended college but didn't graduate. He left school after two years because he wanted to work in the family business.

Our friend has all the traits that ensure success. He would have been successful building his own business had he not inherited it from his father. He has a positive attitude and boundless energy, and he is always enthusiastic. He is a good salesperson who believes in what he is doing; he is concerned about his customers and goes the extra mile for them. He is a good marketer who plans ahead and puts his plans into action. Most important, he is an entrepreneur who pays attention to details, worries a lot, works with a sense of urgency, and is opportunistic.

The electrical company was thriving when he inherited it, so our friend focused his energies on the construction company. Within a few years he had built it to double its size. Through a series of investments in local real estate and development projects, he built a small business into one of the largest corporations in the region.

Buying a Business

If you buy an existing business, you face many of the same challenges of those who inherit their businesses. People expect the business to operate the same way. Or conversely, if the business hasn't been run properly, others expect you to correct the situation. This still puts the onus on you to make it successful.

An example of an entrepreneur who bought his business and developed it far beyond what it had been is another friend, interior designer Carleton Varney. As he relates in his book, *There's No Place Like Home,* he worked for a well-known interior designer, Dorothy Draper. Through a long series of negotiations Carleton acquired the business, and named it Dorothy Draper & Company, Ltd.

Over the next twenty-five years, he successfully expanded his business venture far beyond its original size. In addition, he established more than twenty "Carleton Varney By The Yard" retail stores worldwide, licensed his name for home products such as wallpaper and fabrics, designed a successful line of fine dinnerware, produced a syndicated column, published over twenty books, and founded the Carleton Varney School of Art and Design at the University of Charleston. He exhibits all the traits of the other entrepreneur just described who inherited his business.

Transitions During Takeover

Both business owners mentioned above had trouble during the transition. Other small business buyers describe problems they have when taking over someone else's business. Some customers have to be placated and some employees have to be accommodated during the transition. Sometimes the transition will be a rocky one. The old staffs are used to the old ways of doing things. Our friend with the electrical contracting companies described it as a sweeping away of the old guard. He said, "It's not that the new broom sweeps clean. It's just that whatever needs to be swept out goes out the door during the transition."

Our friend who inherited the business says in his case, the old employees who were set in their ways resisted any changes he instituted. They could not relate to the "young buck" who was taking over and resented any suggestions. Half of the workers welcomed changes and became good employees. The other half did not, and didn't stay. Our friend who bought his business had similar experiences.

Creating a Business

If you create your business yourself, you have the advantage of no previous expectations from others. You set the standard from the beginning. You have no excess baggage to worry about, no dissatisfied customers to placate, no unhappy employees to accommodate, no previous reputation to live down or to live up to. Of course, you have no track record either, so the bank may not feel comfortable with backing you.

My husband and I represent an example of small business owners who started their own businesses. Since most small businesses start this way, I will describe how we got started in more detail. Like most business owners, Gene started our business in the same industry in which he worked. Like most entrepreneurs who become dissatisfied with their jobs, their bosses, or their companies and decide to do something on their own, Gene felt it was time to start our own business.

In our case, the corporation Gene worked for made a sudden decision to discontinue producing the product he was selling, fine china. That meant closing his division. It also meant abandoning his customers. Gene felt an obligation to help the customers but knew he couldn't because the corporation promoted him to director of marketing for another company they owned.

Some of the customers threatened a class action suit against the corporation for abandoning their china line. Gene remembered what the marketing director had said when they closed his division, "We aren't interested in a three million dollar a year business. We aren't interested in a five million dollar a year business, and I'm not sure we're even interested in a ten million dollar a year business." (Remember these are 1974 dollars.) Gene had created that division and built it to three million dollars and a good profit each year.

The Decision to Start

Gene came home from that meeting and said, "Three million may not seem good enough for them, but it's good enough for us." That was the deciding factor that convinced Gene we should start our company. He had three reasons for making that decision: he had a desire to help his customers; he wanted to continue doing what he enjoyed; and he knew the market niche he had been operating in was profitable.

For the next few months he spent evenings and weekends on the telephone talking with customers and searching for other suppliers. Earlier he had investigated the competition in that particular market niche. Gene felt confident we could start a small company to supply decorated dinnerware for direct sales companies by continuing to do what he had been doing for the past ten years.

He was less confident that we could supply the capital to support such a venture. His financial insight protected us from a common pitfall of small business owners — overextending. Gene's concern over our limited finances determined the speed with which we entered the market. He was forced to start our business on a part-time basis, moonlighting.

He worked for the large corporation almost a year and enlisted my help to get us started before he left their employment. After he left, he worked at three part-time jobs simultaneously while running our company. I was teaching part time at three universities and had time to devote to the minor details of running our business.

We were lucky that Gene could conduct all of his business by telephone. We didn't need an office or a showroom, all we needed was Gene's abilities as salesman, marketer, and entrepreneur and my help following through on minor details.

Filling a Need in the Market

A number of small business owners we know started in a similar way. These entrepreneurs see customer needs that are not being satisfied, or they see an opportunity to enter a particular

niche in their industry's market. We have a friend who epitomizes this.

Stan had worked for a number of years as a sales rep for a decal company in our ceramic industry. He was a good salesman
and a good marketer. When his employment situation became
uncomfortable, he decided to start his own business.

Stan knew there was a need for supplying several different
products in the collectibles field. His work with the decal company had revealed an opportunity to supply several different kinds
of customers. In the collectibles market, he had discovered a special niche for collector plates, figurines, and music boxes. He also
discovered other customers in the premium incentive field.

At the same time he became acquainted with manufacturers
of these items in this country and abroad. He did all this while he
was working in the decal business. He knew the industry, the
customers, and the suppliers. He also realized he was ready to fill
a small niche no one was filling.

While Stan was building his business, he worked as a rep for
our company and several others simultaneously. Gene was aware
that Stan was building his company by working for ours and ad-
mired him. I warned Gene that he was teaching Stan concepts
that would help Stan leave us. Gene said, "People are like products. They have a life span too, and you can't extend them beyond
their time." Entrepreneurs appreciate and often help one another.

Stan never left our company while we were owners, although
he could have. We wanted him to replace Gene as CEO when
we sold our company. Stan refused because he wanted to be a
small business owner like Gene, not a salaried CEO working for a
larger group.

Starting Twice

An example of a small business owner who did not achieve
success until his second attempt is my hair stylist, Paul. He
worked several years for other hair salons and developed a good
clientele. Extremely talented, he had the traits of an entrepreneur that would make him successful as a small business owner.

When he became disillusioned with his employer he started
his own business, but it was not successful. Many small business
owners aren't successful the first time for several reasons. They
don't identify their customers, fit the market, or have enough
capital. In Paul's case, he didn't have the capital. He went back
to work for another salon, and several years later when he became disillusioned again he started his own business a second
time. This time Paul took two partners, a talented hair stylist,
Guillermo, who brought his own clientele thereby adding to the

customer base, and an efficient receptionist, Barbara, who had experience working with people. This second venture has been highly successful. As the business has prospered, he has hired other hair stylists who also bring their clientele to add to the customer base.

Paul's case illustrates the added problems some entrepreneurs have getting started. They must make a larger initial investment because of special equipment. These small business owners need to plan carefully, borrow sufficient money, and have a good financial base to be successful.

If your small business requires a specialized building, special equipment, licenses, or skilled help, you need more planning time, more initial capital, and more savings to live on while you get started. Major factors to consider when getting started include: (1) moonlighting, (2) picking partners, (3) husband and wife teams, (4) advisors and consultants, and (5) your role as buyer and seller.

MOONLIGHTING

Most small business owners start their companies on a part-time basis, moonlighting, as we did. Gene was still working for the large corporation, and I was teaching part time at universities. I think it's important to digress for a moment to describe how Gene left the corporation because it demonstrates a special quality I observed in several small business owners. That is the quality of perceiving oneself as successful, confident, and in control of one's destiny, no matter how it may appear to others.

This sense of independence and refusal to accept defeat is a rare quality. Gene demonstrated it when the corporation let him go. It came about when he wrote a marketing plan that showed a better profit picture for the company if Gene's job was eliminated. The company did just that.

After they let him go, it would have been normal for Gene to collect unemployment benefits. Gene refused, saying, "I'm not unemployed. I'm starting my own company." We really needed the money during the first few months our business was getting started. We had a large debt on a country home and guest cottage, 130 acres with 30,000 pine trees to preserve, a pond to maintain, a stable of four horses and kennel of five dogs to feed, and a daughter in graduate school. Despite these responsibilities, Gene refused to collect unemployment benefits. He personified what my father, who built several small businesses, once said, "I've been short of cash, but I have never been out of work."

Consulting to Make Ends Meet

After Gene left the corporation, he took consulting jobs with three different companies to be sure we had a good financial base. He consulted for an American china manufacturer, helping them improve sales in their factory outlet stores that distributed their china. He spent long hours developing a marketing plan for them and traveling to the stores to help implement some of his ideas, and to check on the store managers. I went with him on many of these trips so we could work on our own business plans while traveling. The consulting work gave Gene additional experience in a different segment of the china industry, the factory store end.

He also worked as a consultant for a direct sales company, helping them develop a marketing plan for importing fine porcelain to supply their sales force. This was a good opportunity for Gene to become acquainted with overseas suppliers and the foreign market. It offered us our first trip to Japan. Gene patterned his marketing plan for this company after the one he had developed for the china division at the large corporation.

One of his ideas was developing dinnerware patterns compatible with crystal, flatware, and linen and providing romantic names and stories to accompany them. Of special interest was the creation of pattern names and stories. He wanted the customer to be able to repeat a story that romanticized the tableware pattern.

For example, a china pattern might be called, "Royal Baroness." A short description would be written about the gold filigree border of the china design that was borrowed from a similar design found on the wedding ring of a baroness. It was a good sales technique and helped merchandize the products. Gene and I wrote many of these pattern stories. A friend of our daughter's later wrote them and eventually joined our company as a creative writer.

While consulting for this direct sales company, Gene had an opportunity to test many of his ideas while earning money we badly needed to fund our own company. He also had the opportunity to come in contact with a number of people in the industry and to learn about new suppliers, including box manufacturers, printers, decal makers, and other companies that would be useful for our business later.

His third consulting job was with a Japanese marketing company in New York. Gene wrote a marketing plan and developed a china line for the owner. The porcelain dinnerware was designed for the general consumer and produced in Japan. Although the three companies Gene consulted for were in the tableware industry, the products were slightly different and their markets did not overlap. The American china company was concerned with producing low cost china for factory outlet stores. The direct sales company was marketing china for the direct selling field. The Japanese company was marketing porcelain for the general consumer market. Each of the companies knew that Gene was doing other consulting work in the industry and that he was working to develop his own company.

While working these three jobs, Gene was able to write his own marketing plan for our company and put together a fine china line to supply our first customer, the owner of a direct sales company in Canada. Within another year the Japanese marketing company went out of business, leaving a large unpaid debt to Gene. To compensate, Gene flew to Japan and took over one of their porcelain lines.

The Temptation to Give Up

During this same period, Gene was offered the presidency of the direct sales company for which he was consulting. They offered him more money than he had ever earned and promised him complete control of the new company. The offer was tempting, but not for long.

When Gene asked my opinion, I told him I would rather sell our home and everything we had and move back to an apartment than see him working for someone else again. He was fifty, and we both knew if we were going to start a business it had to be right then. We turned down the offer and never regretted it.

What happened to us is not unusual. We have talked with other small business owners who have said that after starting their own business someone offered them the deal of a lifetime. Some succumbed to the temptation and were sorry. Others were not sorry, nevertheless remaining wistful about the company they gave up.

The owner of the direct sales company that offered Gene the presidency died within two years of the job offer, and the company was dissolved. If Gene had abandoned his dream for the job offer, he would have been looking for a job in a short time. Unless circumstances demand that a person give up his or her new company, it is usually not a good idea to abandon a dream. People we have known who have done so have most often regretted it. George Bernard Shaw said, "Take care to get what you like or you will be forced to like what you get."

Families Are Important

If you decide to continue with your new company, it will require complete cooperation and enthusiasm from your family members or it won't work. In fact, all of the successful entrepreneurs we know have very supportive families. Our informal poll indicates that if the family isn't behind him or her 100 percent, the entrepreneur is quite likely to have several spouses during his or her lifetime.

Many spouses are not able to accept all the changes and risks that occur when living with an entrepreneur, especially one who is operating a small business. The risk alone is frightening. Spouses have to be wholly committed to the project to understand the hours they will spend alone. It is imperative they either work in the business too or have a keen interest in something of their own.

If the business owner is a female, an ego problem may develop for her spouse. Male spouses of successful women like Debbie Fields, of Mrs. Fields Cookies, are special people with very secure egos. Female spouses also have to feel secure as individuals to avoid feeling left out and alone.

If you have the complete support of your spouse and family, continue working as many jobs as you can to support yourselves while you get your company started. If you can work in industries that are closely associated with what you want to do, it will be easier for you and certainly contribute to building networks that can be useful to you later.

Honesty Pays Dividends

A word of caution: never do anything to exploit the companies for which you are working. Never take their customers, their lists, or anything that even borders on being dishonest. Tell them about your own company and what you are planning, if you can. Gene told the companies he was consulting for, and they proved to be helpful.

You may find one of the company's employees is doing the same thing. One small business owner we know found his partner that way. When each of them learned the other was interested in setting up his own glass decorating plant, they formed a partnership. One had marketing skills and the other had manufacturing and personnel skills. There were no hard feelings when one partner left the company to go with our friend who was consulting for them. The partners established a small glass decorating plant and are quite successful.

PICKING PARTNERS

Most small business owners don't have partners. That's because entrepreneurs tend to be loners instead of team players. They don't need people around to get the job done. Sometimes they feel people just get in the way. They don't feel they need a partner in their business and will avoid it if they can. However, circumstances may force them to consider taking a partner.

Decide with Caution to Fill a Need

If you have been thinking about taking a partner, think very carefully. Be sure you really need to have a partner and then proceed with caution. Let's review reasons for taking a partner, and then look at some reasons partnership may not be such a good idea.

There are really only two reasons for taking a partner: to raise capital, and to acquire more management or technical skills for the business. If you need money, you should exhaust all the ways to obtain a loan before entering into a partnership to get it. If you present your business plan to your local banker, the Small Business Administration, or other government agencies, you may get the capital you require. You can always look for venture capitalists or an investor who will loan you the money or invest in your business without requiring you to enter into a partnership, other than a limited one.

If you have selling and marketing skills but you are weak in management skills, you may need help. Even if you have all those skills, you may still need help if you are not acquainted with some technical aspect of your industry. But needing help does not necessarily mean needing a partner. You may be able to hire the help you need. Two heads are not necessarily better than one. You may end up at loggerheads.

On the positive side, if it's capital you're after, taking a partner will double your money, or augment it, immediately. Sharing the financial responsibilities of the business will make it easier and less risky. In the best sense, it means someone else is committed to the success of the business as much as you are. It also means someone else is working as hard as you are to make money for the business. But be aware also that now the business has two people to support rather than one; sometimes this added burden is too much for a new business.

A Good Partner

If you are lucky, you may get a partner whose only interest in the business is financial. In that case, the partner will more than likely remain a silent partner and let you run the business. We had a silent partner when we started our manufacturing operation. We had been successfully operating the marketing firm for a year or two before we started the manufacturing plant.

Starting a manufacturing operation is more costly. It requires a building, machinery, supporting materials, and all the overhead that goes along with a skilled labor force. We needed a great deal more money than we could supply or borrow, so we took a silent partner.

For a year we operated with this partner. He was the best partner anyone could have. Even with a perfect partner, there was a heavy burden on Gene. He spent a lot of time on the telephone keeping the partner updated on all our activities. I'm sure Gene spent more time than he needed to, but he felt obligated to cover every detail of what we had just done or were planning to do.

Before long Gene noticed that we had more money invested in the manufacturing business than our partner had, yet Gene was spending additional time keeping him apprised of all our activities and splitting everything down the middle. That's when we bought him out.

In our case it worked out fine. Our friend was happy because he made a handsome return on his short-term investment. We were happy because he helped us get started with our manufacturing operation. We were also happy to be completely on our own with both our marketing firm and the manufacturing operation. We were no longer tied up in a partnership, except with each other. We were lucky.

Partners and Personalities

My hairdresser, Paul, was lucky when he found Guillermo and Barbara as partners. Their personalities and lifestyles are compatible and intertwined. They have developed a good relationship, combining their traits to form a solid business partnership. They truly complement one another. Such partnerships are rare.

Choosing a partner for your business is a serious step. You need to be careful and be sure your partner complements you in as many ways as possible. It is better for the business and for both of you if your partner's skills compensate for your deficiencies and vice versa. Compatible skills make everything run more smoothly.

It is just as important for your personality traits to be compatible. Sometimes those traits you admire in a person from a distance are not as admirable up close, in day-to-day situations. You may admire a person's aggressiveness in business situations until that aggression is turned on you. Then you may resent it. Or you may admire a person's tendency to acquiesce to your wishes, until you find that person does the same to everyone. Then you may view it as a weakness.

Entering into a partnership is a lot like getting married. You take each other for better or for worse, and sometimes worse will be the case. People change over the years, and a person who may seem fine to you now may not be fine later. People can develop family problems, drinking problems, or other problems that become *your* problems. You may find you don't get along with your partner's family members and that can cause a problem.

Setting Ground Rules

It is important to set some ground rules in any partnership. It is usually wise not to socialize with your business partner. The most successful partnerships are generally strictly business. While a once a year get-together may be appropriate for any business relationship, weekly, monthly, or periodic parties are not wise. To use a tired clich, familiarity does sometimes breed contempt. We never socialized with our partner, as much as we liked him and his wife.

Aside from personality traits that can cause problems, seats of authority can cause other problems. That is why it is important to set parameters early, and formally, to know who is responsible for what. If it is a fifty-fifty partnership, you still need to formally acknowledge who is responsible for managing the personnel, the marketing, and the finances.

Your attorney should draw up a partnership agreement that defines all aspects of your relationship so there are no questions about these responsibilities. There can be no secrets between partners. Each of you is an agent of the business, and each of you is accountable to the other during the course of your partnership.

Agreements and Disagreements

To further protect yourself, it is wise to have your partnership agreement state the methods to be used in the event you want to buy out your partner or vice versa. You should address any problems you can think of that might arise, for instance, whether both of you are liable in equal amount for losses, whether each of your personal properties can be attached by creditors, how the proceeds are divided if the business is sold, and what happens when one of you dies. There are a number of questions that need to be answered before you enter into a partnership. These are just a few of them.

A word of caution. Whether your partner is a friend, a family member, or someone you have just met, be sure you set guidelines for who will have the final say in a dispute. This is especially necessary for family members. Three cases here illustrate what business and personal problems can occur if you don't set such guidelines. The first case is not a family partnership; the other two are.

We have a friend who is a minority stockholder in a partnership. Our friend is more knowledgeable about the day-to-day operations of the business than the other partner. Yet our friend must always yield to the decisions of the partner even though the partner sometimes makes decisions that are wrong for the business.

Their company has missed some good opportunities due to the more powerful partner's inability to assess the market correctly. The company has also made some mistakes with clients, giving too much credit, because our friend's partner was too trusting and didn't follow our friend's advice. (This misadventure is described in more detail when I discuss disasters.)

A case involving a family is a partnership of brothers who inherited their business from their father, a successful entrepreneur. One brother is in charge of manufacturing. The other brother takes care of the marketing for the company. The brother who runs the manufacturing end of the business feels he must get full support from the other brother before making decisions because the other brother is older and maintains a familial control over him. This has caused business and family problems at different times.

The other family case involves two brothers who eventually had a falling out that has never been mended despite their parents' futile attempts to bring them back together. The family breakup occurred because there was a business disagreement that escalated into a family feud with the father originally taking sides. Many years later, the brothers are still not speaking even though the father has made up with both sons and has attempted to mend the rift.

HUSBAND AND WIFE TEAMS

A number of successful small businesses are owned and operated by husband and wife teams. Ours was. Before you undertake that venture, do some serious thinking. The riskiest type of partnership is the husband and wife type. It is riskiest because when this type of partnership doesn't work, you stand to lose both your business and your spouse. The rest of this chapter could be filled with case studies of husband and wife business teams that didn't work out. For every one that is successful, there are twice as many that are not. Business is risky. So is marriage. When you combine the two, you have not doubled the problem you have squared it. However, if it works, you can have twice as much fun and make twice as much money.

Ground Rules that Work

We have known several successful husband and wife partnerships. They all follow the same basic common sense guidelines we followed to protect both our marriage and our business relationship. If you are thinking about forming such a partnership with your spouse, I suggest you follow these guidelines. They will work for you too.

First, you need to have a sincere belief in the other person, both emotionally and intellectually. You need to trust the other person completely and believe that your spouse truly cares about you and about the business. One of you will probably be more deeply involved in the business than the other, but not much, if it's going to work. Both of you need to be fully committed to the business and to each other.

You have to trust each other's judgment. For years Gene had to travel while I stayed home with our daughter. That was the loneliest period in both our lives. Gene hated to travel. I enjoy traveling and would have preferred to travel. Gene would have preferred to stay home. He vowed that as soon as we could afford it I would go on every business trip with him—and I have.

Gene and I often thought companies purposely send dedicated family men on the road. They know those men will do the job well and as rapidly as possible so they can come home and not have to make follow-up trips. That saves companies money. When we owned our company, we found ourselves feeling the same way. Now that women are working in similar jobs, I believe the same reasoning is valid for them.

Not wanting to travel alone anymore was one of the motivating factors in making our business successful as quickly as possible. Gene dreaded it so much that traveling together was one of the first priorities on our agenda. He insisted I go on every business trip and I was glad to join him.

Before we started our manufacturing operation, I traveled some in my own field while Gene stayed home. We both enjoyed that arrangement more than the other one. However, after I joined the firm full time and we traveled together, we both agreed that was the best arrangement of all.

Mixing Business with Pleasure

If you are a husband and wife team and travel together, try to mix business with pleasure while you are traveling. Owners who are dedicated to their businesses work as hard and as many hours as they can in a day. That is good and necessary for success. However, you also need some time for yourself and for each other. Being in a different place together gives you the opportunity to discover new things together. Gene hated traveling alone because he didn't enjoy seeing anything new if I wasn't there to share it with him. If you have a good marriage you each feel that way.

Traveling on business can provide you with opportunities to enjoy each other outside work hours. Since I have many varied interests, Gene relied on me to set the itinerary for these short sightseeing excursions. I always made sure we spent time at a museum, ballet, concert, or the theater. We enjoyed some limited sightseeing and a limited amount of shopping in every country we visited. Sometimes Gene planned fly-fishing trips for us when our business took us to certain areas. If you enjoy each other's company, working together in business is an ideal arrangement.

You need to be meticulous with your record-keeping to be sure you separate legitimate business expenses from your personal expenditures. You have an obligation to do this because you are part of a team that includes all of your employees. If you have a profit-sharing program, as we did, you have an additional reason to be as honest as you can with your company expenses. You want to have as much profit as possible to share. As small business owners, you set the example by your attitude and your behavior. If you expect your people to be honest with their expense reports, you need to be honest with yours.

Many direct sales companies foster husband and wife teams. Some direct sales companies recognize the woman as the pivotal person in the team. In these cases, the husband works in an ancillary position. Other companies rely on the husband to be the driving force and count on the wife to work at supportive jobs.

Who Is in Charge?

The husband and wife partnership works best when you define who is in charge at the beginning. Whether the husband or wife plays the major role is not as important as defining and mutually accepting who the major role player is. You may each have equal power in your end of the business, but when a final countdown occurs you have to know who is boss. It is also perfectly acceptable for the person in charge to change from one partner to the other in different circumstances. The important thing is to mutually know and mutually accept the arrangement.

In our case, if the problem involved manufacturing or personnel, the final decision was usually mine. If the problem involved marketing or finances, the final decision was usually Gene's. We never argued over who was making the decision or what it would be, though we sometimes argued over how to handle it. Most decisions we made jointly.

In addition to laying the ground rules, believing and trusting in each other, being totally committed to the business, and knowing who is in charge, it is necessary to keep things in perspective. That means playing fair by leaving your business disagreements at the office and your personal disputes at home. Never carry over from one domain to the other. It is not only in poor taste, it is poor business judgment.

People who observed us disagreeing during a business discussion were often surprised at our ability to leave the meeting as friends. Employees who worked closely with us were amazed that we could disagree so vociferously at times and maintain our equilibrium toward each other afterward.

On occasion, we disagreed about details regarding how to handle situations that developed with certain customers. We also disagreed about how to handle a temperamental designer who wanted also to act as a rep for us. He worked for us briefly, but during that period Gene and I battled frequently over how to handle him and what to do with him. We were both relieved when we finally severed our business relationship with him. When he joined another company, he caused the same problems with them.

If you are wondering who won when we disagreed, it was never a question of who won or lost, or who was right or wrong. It was always a question of what was best for the business. We both viewed it that way. That was why both of us could compromise and one acquiesce one time and the other do the same another time. You need to be able to do this, if your husband and wife partnership is going to work.

Admit Mistakes and Don't Interfere

This reminds me of another attribute you need to succeed as a husband and wife team—admitting mistakes. Admitting mistakes was one of the major requirements of all our employees and a part of our value system. I discuss it in more detail in the next chapter under goal setting and quality control. If you can admit your mistakes without losing your sense of self worth, you will find it easier to work as a husband and wife business team. It also helps to have a sense of humor.

Finally, I think you have to respect the other person and his or her ability to do the job. It is critical that you stay in your area of expertise. Never try to take over the other person's job. You can give advice and should, if it's asked for or if you see a need. But perceive it as that—advice, not an order. I believe more husband and wife partnerships dissolve because of interference in the other person's job than for any other single reason.

A Sense of Humor Helps

Handle interference with grace and courtesy, and occasionally a sense of humor. Here is an example. Shortly after I took over the manufacturing operation, I noticed Gene coming to the inspection table asking inspectors why they had rejected certain pieces. He could see nothing wrong with the items. The inspectors became concerned and thought they should seek his permission before discarding things.

When I discovered what he was doing, I asked him to stay in the front office and out of the plant. I reminded him that he would not like it if I called his customers and started second guessing his work with them. He understood but still found it difficult to see us discard items he thought we could ship. He was not as acquainted with the quality standards we had set as those of us in the plant were.

I finally instructed our workers and supervisors to call me whenever he went to the back of the plant. They did, so I followed him, and in a friendly, humorous way I reminded him of our agreement. We are both nearsighted, so I teased him, saying neither of us was qualified to be inspectors and pointed out that was why we were lucky to have such well-trained employees who did see flaws we couldn't see. We all approached it with a sense of humor, and within a short period he quit going to the inspection area.

For all the problems that can arise with a husband and wife team, if you approach the partnership carefully, set the guidelines, and are honest throughout the trial period, it can work. If you find it doesn't, look on it as a learning experience and don't let it affect your personal relationship. No business is worth that. If you have a good, solid relationship, keep that and get a different business partner.

ADVISORS AND CONSULTANTS

You may not need a partner to succeed as a business owner, but you need advisors and consultants at different times. Be careful when you select them and use only the ones you need. Whether you begin using advisors at the beginning or later, you will need them. We relied on three at the beginning—our banker, our attorney, and our CPA. Later, when we started our manufacturing operation, we used several outside consultants to help train our people. For the duration of our ownership, we relied on consultants, freelance artists, and advisors.

A Financial Advisor

Most small business owners have some background in basic accounting procedures. Unless you have more than high school, trade school, or college accounting training, you need a financial advisor. Gene studied accounting in business college and later at a university. Yet he did not rely on himself to set up our accounting procedures or to maintain our books. He always used an outside accounting firm with a CPA.

The financial advice you get can be invaluable no matter what type of small business you own. Gene relied heavily on our accounting firm. Even though he was meticulous in his record-keeping, he felt more secure knowing a CPA was auditing our books each year. Our bank was more comfortable also, because of the heavy debt we carried. Good financial records document your activities for tax purposes, help you monitor your operating performance, and give you information about the financial state of your business.

Do not wait until you are officially operating your business before keeping accurate records. From the beginning, you need to document everything you declare as business expenses. You can't do that with scraps of paper, scribbled notes, and your memory. You need to set up a system to compile, record, and analyze all your business data.

A Legal Advisor

Another business advisor you need is an attorney, whether you start your business as a sole proprietorship, a partnership, or a corporation. We started as a sole proprietorship with a DBA form (doing business under an assumed name). After a year or so, we formed a partnership with an investor to obtain money for our manufacturing plant. Within a year we bought him out and formed a second corporation. We had already changed our sole proprietorship to a corporation for our marketing firm.

Most small business owners have a family attorney. Many rely on them to provide the legal work for doing business. Unless your attorney has special training in corporate law, I suggest you get additional legal counsel for your business.

Our family attorney was an estate lawyer. When we told him we wanted to start our own business, he recommended the services of another attorney in the law firm who specialized in corporate work. When we needed advice about unions, we obtained the services of a labor relations attorney in Pittsburgh.

If your business requires licenses for products you make, import, or export, you need an attorney who specializes in those areas of the law. If you deal with government agencies, seek the services of an attorney acquainted with them.

We bid for a government contract once. The paperwork was extensive, yet the contract was not sufficient for the work it entailed. We learned that through a technicality our bid was not considered and our time and effort were wasted. If you decide to work for government contracts get good counsel first and be prepared for mounds of paperwork and a long waiting period before you get the contract. We decided we didn't need government contracts to exist.

Checking Credentials Is Important

Take responsibility for yourself and your business even if you get good legal and financial counsel. And don't be afraid to change advisors. The first accountant we got was recommended by our banker so we didn't check his credentials. Gene only used him one time and said he was so uninformed, so unqualified, and so confused that during the presentation of Gene's first financial proposal to the bank Gene was embarrassed. He never used that accountant again.

Learn from our experience: check credentials carefully and interview any advisors who are recommended to you, no matter who recommended them. Ask for references before you hire. Don't be intimidated or believe everything they tell you if your common sense tells you otherwise. Any mistakes they make in giving you incorrect advice hurt you more than they do them. They only get fired. You may get fined, or worse.

That is why Gene spent money only on good accounting and legal firms and none on marketing consultants. Several people wanted to consult for us after we became visibly successful. One man wanted $1000 a day as a marketing consultant. He had been a vice president for a large conglomerate and had a manufacturing background. Naturally, Gene turned him down. I suggest you do too, if someone wants to help you do what you do best. If you need that kind of help, don't start your business.

Shortly after we started our business, we used a consulting firm specializing in personnel matters to handle an unemployment dispute, and we lost the case. We decided then to learn how to handle our own unemployment cases. We did a better job and never used their services again. Later we used an attorney for a more complicated unemployment case and lost it. What few cases we had we handled ourselves. We believe we did a better job because we knew all the details and could relate them with more conviction since we had a vested interest in the outcome.

A Board of Directors

If you have a corporation, you need to have a board of directors meeting regularly. Our corporate attorney suggested we have a monthly board meeting, discuss at least one business issue, and write minutes of the meeting. We wrote the minutes together, Gene signed as board president and I signed as secretary. We always conducted the meeting over dinner at a nice restaurant. It was a special treat to ourselves from the corporation. It also established credibility and left a record in case we ever wanted to sell, although that was not our intention at the time.

Our board of directors included the two of us, although our daughter served as a board member when she was active in the business for a short time. We did not want any other board members. Most small business owners we know do not want or need outside board members. Use your common sense. If you feel you need additional counsel, or financial support that might result from including other board members, include them. Include only those people who can make a significant contribution. It is best not to include people who are on the payroll or who already give you advice.

We tried to follow the suggestions of our business advisors. We found they were an asset and worth the money we paid them. An advantage to using professional advisors is their knowledge in special areas. The nature of your business will determine the type of advisors you need.

YOU AS BUYER AND SELLER

To be a successful business owner, you need to play a dual role. You are somebody's customer and you are somebody's supplier.

Select Good Suppliers

Your product or service depends on the resources you use. Therefore, you have to be a wise shopper. If you want to produce a fine product, you need good components. That means you must have good suppliers. Your first step is to compile a library of sources. It can be as small as a single catalog, a special issue from an industry magazine, or several different catalogs from several sources. You also need a list compiled from your personal contacts in the industry. You need a choice of suppliers for all of the products you use in your business.

Study the catalogs and lists, call suppliers, and learn what items they supply and the quality of those items. You need good components to turn out a good product. Learn how high their standards are. Make sure they operate with the same standards you do.

Once you have established that their quality is what you want, ask them what their policies are for deliveries and replacements. Will they deliver on time and consistently? If you must order in larger quantities than you can immediately use, will they give you delayed billing terms? Will they warehouse for you? If you need replacements will they provide them promptly? Can you afford to wait? Will you lose your customers as we did on occasion?

When we first started our business, we used an English supplier for some of our porcelain. We lost customers when we couldn't meet delivery dates because of the time it took the supplier to replace bad merchandise from their original shipments. It wasn't our fault. Or was it? We thought because we were getting our components from one of the top porcelain manufacturers in England, we would have no problems. But we did.

When you select a supplier, you also need to know who will service the account, how reliable they are, and how sensitive they are to your needs. When you have problems with reps, report them to their companies and ask for help. Anytime a vendor's rep doesn't give you the service you need, take action.

When you order samples, use them in controlled situations first to evaluate them before integrating them totally into your process. You can't be too careful. Don't order huge quantities until you have given the product a good test in your workplace, with your people, under your working conditions.

Finally, go to as many seminars relating to the products you buy as you can. The more you learn about your suppliers and what they can do for you, the better your product will be. Every time an association offers workshops, attend or send someone from your company. You will improve your operation and your product by keeping up to date on the latest developments. Trade shows also offer opportunities to meet suppliers and attend seminars. (These are discussed in more detail in Chapter 4.)

Provide a Good Workplace

What are your responsibilities as a seller? You probably know but let's review them. You need to get a good product or service out the door, on time and at a fair price. That means you have to have a good workplace and a good workforce. If you have taken the steps suggested above, you have the best components you can get. You are buying from good suppliers who will give you good delivery and make replacements when necessary. You have made sure your suppliers are sending you a good rep who will provide good service. And you are keeping up to date on the latest products and procedures by reading and attending workshops. Now you have the basis for creating a good product.

Your job is to produce it at a fair price. To do that you need to make sure you study the market and know what a fair price is. Check your competition. Check your own organization too. You need to provide the best environment you can for your workers. Make sure you have instituted all the possible labor-saving devices so your workers can do their jobs efficiently. Include your workers in the planning stages of any new procedures that affect them and they will have a vested interest in making those procedures work. Integrate your workers in the total operation of your company and they will have more concern for your product and your company. Their total involvement will be reflected in superior job performances. All of this will save you money and result in a better product.

You need to be sure you are giving adequate training so that new workers, or workers trying new jobs, learn the proper way to do their jobs. Do cross-training so workers can fill in for coworkers in an emergency. In addition to good training, you need to maintain good daily work habits. A major part of those daily work habits must include admitting and reporting mistakes. You can't produce a good product if you don't catch the mistakes in-house before the product is shipped. Inspecting the product at different stages of production helps, but it doesn't solve the problem of quality control. You still need the cooperation of your workers to make sure you are turning out a good product at a fair price.

You also need the full cooperation of your workers to make sure your product is delivered on time. People work best in a clean, safe environment where policies are implemented consistently and fairly. They also work best when they can measure their achievements and feel rewarded for individual effort. Offer bonuses and awards for individual and group effort. Set production schedules carefully and plan for emergencies; you will minimize the problem of making deliveries on time. You will meet your responsibilities as a customer and a supplier if you take these common sense measures.

DEALING WITH COMPETITION

Whenever your business is down and you think the problem is the competition, think again. The problem is never the competition. The problem is how you respond to it. You can complain about the competition and use it as an excuse for a decline in your business, or you can respond by using the competition as a challenge to do better. Competition is good; it proves there is a market for your product, and it keeps the marketplace interested in your kind of product. Without competition, there would be no market.

I have a positive attitude toward competition because our competitors put us in business, taught us many things we used in our operation, and sent us customers from time to time. When we started our company, we believed there was room for all of us in a growing, thriving industry. There still is.

Complaining about the competition is not the answer. The answer lies in doing four things: finding your niche in the market, learning from your competitors, working with your competitors, and having a positive attitude.

The first, finding your niche in the market, means knowing what *you* want to do, then being the best at it. Knowing who your customer is, what your customer wants, and keeping focused on satisfying your customer. It means finding where you fit in an expanding, changing market created by the competition. Remember, if there is competition there is a market. Your competitors help create that market.

Have you ever noticed when a fast food restaurant opens on a busy street that several more open on the same street soon afterward? Often they open side by side. Before long there is a restaurant strip. They are all competitors and they all do a good business. Why? Because each has found its niche in the market and offers something slightly different, slightly better, or slightly cheaper. Each knows who their customer is and satisfies that customer. Notice too that they each add new products, meeting a changing market.

Find your particular niche in the market and exploit it. Here is an analogy based on what is taught in anthropology. Species survive, even thrive, over long periods of time based on their ability to exploit an ecological niche from the general environment. For millions of years, small lizards thrived in the same general environment as huge dinosaurs because they exploited different ecological niches.

So too small companies thrive in the same general industrial environment as giants because they exploit different niches. Your size and your flexibility give you the ability to do things giants can't or won't do. You can scurry faster to outrun recessions, change directions rapidly to meet a changing market, maintain higher quality standards with fewer workers, meet faster delivery dates with tighter controls, and give personalized service.

When we owned our company, we believed it was our small size that accounted in large measure for our success. How dare we, a little lizard, compete with the giant dinosaurs, Shenango, Franciscan, and Lenox. Yet today, just eighteen years later, two of these three giants are extinct while the little lizard is still scurrying and thriving. Why? Because a company, any company, can exploit a different market niche and succeed.

To do that, you must keep focused on your customer's needs, and when those needs change you must adapt as the fast food restaurants do. That means realizing that each product has a life. To try and sell a product beyond its time is frustrating and useless. Instead, it's more important to keep a vigilant eye on the changing market and be aware of how and where your particular expertise fits. In other words, keep an eye on your ecological niche without trying to hang on to products your customers no longer want.

The second answer to meeting the challenge of competition is to learn from your competitors. When we visited some of our suppliers overseas who were also our competitors, we never asked them to slow down so that we could compete. We learned from them. We told our workers about our competitors' production quotas, and used their accomplishments as challenges to do better—and we did.

When visiting any competitor here or overseas, discuss personnel policies. Learn how others in the industry hire, manage, and train employees. This can be a great asset when setting up your own operation or streamlining your policies. Observe how others utilize machines and personnel; how they use space, store supplies, or set up work flow.

Communicating and sharing ideas doesn't mean telling trade secrets. If you are working on a new project with a client, you don't discuss it with anyone. This is privileged information. But sharing basic techniques and general information is necessary for companies and industries if they want to thrive and grow.

A third way to meet the challenge of competition is to share projects with competitors when you can. Recommend others when you can't do something. Later, they will reciprocate and recommend you. We did. If they were overseas competitors, we tried to place the project with another American company first. Usually when you can show a customer that American manufacturers can give better delivery dates, better quality, and a "Made in USA" label, these advantages help to offset a lower price.

There is a fourth and final way to meet the challenge of competition. It is the most important way to make sure you meet any challenge. This was discussed in detail in Chapter 1, but I want to emphasize it again. This concept is having a positive attitude about your business, yourself, and life in general.

Thousands of years ago, the Hindus taught the same thing by saying, "A thought becomes an act, an act becomes a habit, a habit develops a character, and a character reaps a destiny." This is a good way of saying you create your own destiny by your attitude. How you think so you act, so you become, and so things happen to you. If you find yourself worrying about losing business because of your competitors, replace that worry with positive images of gaining more business because you are different from your competitors.

Remember, instead of complaining about the competition when business is down, use it as a challenge to do better. Find your niche in the market, learn from your competitors, work with your competitors, and have a positive attitude. I guarantee your business will improve.

3.

Setting Goals

Successful business owners set goals for themselves and for their companies. Many small businesses fail because the owners have not defined their goals clearly. We have a friend who is talented in manufacturing and industrial relations. Twice he has started a small business and twice he has failed. He has just started another small business, manufacturing china. He has adequate financing and plenty of good help. Yet he will not be in business by the time you read this. He is doomed to fail again. I don't know why his other two businesses failed. I do know why his latest venture will. He doesn't know who his customer is. He only has a vague idea. Although he says he has a business plan and a financial plan, it is clear he does not have a marketing plan. He has not defined his goals, who his customers are, and how he will reach them.

We have another friend who wanted us to invest in his idea for a new direct sales jewelry company. Our friend is an excellent salesman with a strong background in sales training and sales management. When he approached us with his idea, he had already formed a partnership with a woman who was also a top sales person with sales management experience. Neither of them had a background in finance or marketing.

Gene asked him to write a basic plan outlining their ideas for marketing the product along with one-year and three-year pro formas. We were surprised when our friend was unable to do so. He talked enthusiastically at great length about his ideas, but he could not commit them to paper. He could never clearly define his goals, consequently he was never able to find an investor to back his idea.

Other small business owners may have definite goals when they start their company but lose sight of them later. We have known several small business owners who have started their companies and done well the first five or six years. Instead of staying with what they do best, they have tried to move into other products or new markets without defining their goals first. They have hurt or destroyed their businesses. They could have made the transition from one segment of the market to another if they had remained aware of their goals and consciously adapted them to fit a changing market.

Goals Change

You can change your goals, adopt new ones, and adapt old ones, but you can never lose sight of them. We knew what we wanted to do when we started our marketing company. We had a definite and clear goal. We wanted to supply coordinated tableware products to the direct sales industry. Everything we did was directed toward accomplishing that stated goal.

Having specific goals when you start your business does not mean staying with only those goals. You need to add and refine them as circumstances and the market change. When we started our business, our only customers were direct sales customers. Two circumstances forced us to adopt additional goals. The first was our suppliers' inability to keep pace with Gene's sales. He was relying on suppliers in Japan and the United States. The American manufacturers were so far behind in their deliveries, Gene decided to start our own china decorating plant.

Adding a decorating plant to our business added another goal —importing undecorated china, called "blanks," from England and Japan and decorating it ourselves. We retained our other goals of importing and selling decorated ware from Japan and selling ware decorated for us by other American companies. The country in which the majority of the cost of a product is generated is considered the country of origin. Thus, most of our china was labeled an American product even though some of the blanks came from another country.

The second circumstance that contributed to Gene's decision to add a decorating facility was the expanding market in the collectibles industry. What had been a small market for a generation was rapidly growing into a multimillion dollar business. There was a great need for more decorating plants to meet the demand. With that as added incentive, Gene was convinced our new venture would be profitable.

Adding this new facility meant setting additional goals. We would supply two markets—direct sales and collectibles. One of our companies would remain a marketing firm while the other one would be a manufacturing firm. Now that we were going to produce a portion of what we supplied, we had to be more specific about defining our quality standards during the production process.

We had agreed earlier that our quality standards would be high to meet the demands of the direct sales customers. Contrary to what many people believe, products sold in the home usually have to meet *higher* quality standards than those sold in retail stores. Home buyers are more critical of products sold in the home partly because they have more opportunity to scrutinize the product. They are also more critical because they have more faith in retail stores they can visit anytime.

One of our major goals from the beginning was supplying a high quality product. Such a goal is not always easy to meet, especially at the beginning. There is a learning curve in most anything you undertake. We had an additional problem because we made a mistake by hiring the wrong person to run the plant when it started. After a short and trying time he left. I joined the company full time, reorganized the manufacturing operation and ran it. (This episode is described under "Disasters.")

When I took over, the first thing I noticed was the lack of focus in the manufacturing operation. My first job was to make certain the kinds of goals Gene had set for the marketing company would be supported by the goals of the manufacturing company.

Goals are important for the small business and critical if you are manufacturing. When setting goals you need to consider: (1) your quality standard, (2) adding company goals, (3) employees, (4) customers, and (5) suppliers here and abroad.

YOUR QUALITY STANDARD

To be successful, a small business must maintain its quality standards while meeting production schedules. The first decision you need to make is how high to set your quality standard. No one can tell you how to do that. Only you can do that. Once you have made that decision, you need to give a precise definition and description of that standard and then decide what you have to do to institute it and maintain it.

Advantages and Disadvantages of a Lower Standard

Whether you set a very high standard for your company or a less rigid one, you need to examine the advantages and disadvantages. If you decide on a less rigid standard, the standard will be easier to maintain. Production will be faster and less expensive because you can reject fewer pieces. You can hire a less qualified person and function adequately with a less rigid training program.

You don't have the added expense of enforcing stringent rules to maintain a very high quality standard. And you can sell your product at a cheaper price, giving you a broader customer base.

There are some disadvantages to a less rigid quality standard. The cheaper selling price means you need to produce more items to meet your operating costs. You may spend more time with customer complaints and, if you are in a labor-intensive business as we were, you need to hire and train many more people to meet the increased production the cheaper prices require.

Advantages and Disadvantages of a Higher Standard

If you set a very high quality standard you can command a higher price for your product, which means you can sell fewer items to satisfy your operating expenses. You can function with a smaller labor force and insist on a higher caliber employee who will probably be easier to train and manage.

If you have a very high quality product, you will probably do business with prestigious customers, which will give you a high status in your community and your industry. Your high quality product will also bring you awards and free publicity, making it easier to market what you produce.

There are some disadvantages to setting a very high quality standard. You limit your customers with your higher selling price. Higher prices are necessary because it is more costly to maintain higher quality standards from the standpoint of hiring and training employees, buying higher quality components, and enforcing tighter inspection standards. Strict quality control may mean rejecting more items.

Instituting and Maintaining Any Standard

Whatever quality standard you decide is best for your company, there are several things you need to do to institute and maintain that standard. You need to hire the right people and give them good training. You need to show employees examples of how quality standards slide if daily care is not taken to maintain good work habits.

If you are going to maintain a high quality standard for the product, you need to insist on the same high quality standard in everything you do that supports that product. For example, you need to maintain a high quality standard in your housekeeping and your office procedures, the letters your secretaries type, the shipments your packers prepare, the warehouse your supervisor manages, and the grounds your maintenance crew services.

Your sales service employees have to reflect that same high quality when they talk with customers, reps, and suppliers. When customers call about price quotes, product information, or shipment dates, your staff has to be prompt, courteous, and eager to help. Your staff must be ready and eager to answer those questions. They must be helpful in getting information as fast as they can. When they promise customers they will get back to them, they need to do so promptly. When they can't, they need to call anyway and explain why not. A high quality sales service staff is one of your most important marketing tools, especially if you want to project a high quality image.

The same goes for all of your employees, especially those who deal with your customers, suppliers, bank, accounting firm, or other outside personnel. The image they project as members of your company reflects on all of you. Their attitude and behavior show others what your standards are.

Even if you settle for a less rigid standard, you still need good people working for you and you need to maintain a good, clean, well-organized work environment and be consistent with your housekeeping. You also need to plan for frequent quality control meetings. If your standard is very high, you may even need daily meetings in some departments. If your standard is less rigid, you can operate with less frequent meetings, but they are still necessary.

How We Maintained a High Standard

Two years after I began running our manufacturing operation we decided, as part of our marketing strategy, to move to as high a quality standard as possible. We realized at the time that the decision to move to such high quality would cost us some customers because higher quality automatically means higher prices.

We soon found the higher prices were offset by the higher status we gained with our clients and with the industry in general. Producing a higher quality product also gave us the opportunity to work with more prestigious accounts. We enjoyed the magazine articles that were written about our work and the international awards we received for excellence in design and decorating techniques.

Instill Pride in Workers

We did several things to instill pride in our employees, which helped maintain a high quality standard. We displayed many of our finished products on the walls of the employee lunchroom. We showed employees papers, brochures, magazine articles, photographs, and other publicity items relating to the china they produced. We hung all awards we received in the general work area to help motivate employees and to impress visitors. We pointed with pride to these awards when we took customers, suppliers, and our banker through the plant. It showed everyone we were a goal-oriented company with high quality standards.

We provided the best atmosphere we could afford for all areas of the workplace. We insisted on meticulous housekeeping. Our floors were scrubbed and polished every night—even in the warehouse of our plant. We did not permit food or beverages in the work areas, and we had a no-smoking policy—even for visitors.

Another way we controlled quality was by keeping samples of each item being produced readily available for study by inspectors. These samples represented different defects that were not acceptable. Each custom project tended to have certain quality problems, oftentimes unique to that project. When we started a new project, we established the standard with our customer and made sure samples of that standard were always available for inspectors. It was a good marketing device that made them aware of our eagerness to please. Even though we were working with high standards, we found some customers wanted even tighter standards than others.

Reward Workers for Quality and Care

We paid workers for the quality of their work. We also stopped production in any department in which losses rose above a certain percentage. To further control quality during production, our supervisors communicated in writing and verbally, between departments, describing any variations they saw in items being produced. Consequently, problems were solved before they escalated into bigger problems.

We also gave bonuses for reporting mistakes. We approached mistakes from a positive standpoint. We did not denigrate workers for making mistakes; instead, we pointed out that mistakes are a natural part of the learning process. Our approach fostered a desire to be careful and do better. This supported our goal for a high quality product. (There is more about our attitude toward mistakes in a later section.)

We also gave a short written description of accidents that resulted in damaging the product during production. This made each person aware of the need to keep alert for any box or cart that was out of place, because these things cause accidents that can hurt people or damage the product.

All these procedures worked to help set and maintain the quality standard we wanted. These things can work for you too. The only bad quality standard is no quality standard. It results in poor work habits and poor morale. Whatever quality standard you select as your goal, make sure you consciously set one, or you will unconsciously settle for one.

ADDING COMPANY GOALS

A successful small business operates with a series of goals, adopting new ones when necessary, and adapting old ones to keep pace. Earlier I related how we started with a few major goals and adopted others to meet the demands of a changing market. In this section I want to illustrate how adopting just one new major goal can result in a series of goals, and how they overlap and support each other.

Existing Goals Support New Goals

When we decided to fit a specific market niche, we knew we had to have high quality, fast delivery, and good customer service. We also knew we had to add another major goal—innovating new decorating techniques. As a result, we had to use the newest ceramic components and tools and conduct a number of experiments. These new goals had to be added to our existing goals, such as our hiring practices and management policies. What we found was that our existing goals provided an environment conducive to innovating new decorating techniques.

First, we projected a positive attitude toward all company goals so that our employees reflected that same attitude. It does no good if you talk about your goals and how important they are and then treat them lightly yourself or forget about them. The example you set is emulated by everyone who comes in contact with you, including your customer, your banker, your supplier, and your employee.

We were careful about hiring and training people. We preferred people with no experience. We found it was easier to train them in our methods if they didn't have any preconceived notions about what could or could not be done and if they had no lazy work habits to break. In addition, we referred to our decorating facility as a "studio," which implies a clean workplace where beautiful things are created. These existing goals made our employees feel proud of what they did and where they worked.

We were careful also to follow through with our existing management policies. We maintained the same meticulous care in every segment of our operation, from production to accounting. For example, our record-keeping system encompassed everything from the initial request to the approval of fired samples, and finally, the approval of the production run.

We used computers for all of our record-keeping and constantly adapted our goals for the office with improved procedures that kept pace with our growing business. As small business owners, we had to keep pace with the latest technology. We found the more consistent we were about implementing existing policies, the more consistent our workers were in maintaining good work habits conducive to innovating new techniques.

We bought the finest ceramic components we could get, used precise instruments, and worked systematically. We had an ongoing dialogue with suppliers to learn about their newest products. When suppliers gave seminars, we attended them. Many times suppliers came to our facility to give us hands-on instructions to meet these new goals.

We insisted that each department devise and conduct some experiment every twelve weeks. The experiment might be anything from arranging items differently for kiln firing to mixing colors, or using various screen meshes in decal production. We maintained a systematic procedure for the review and evaluation of each experiment. We had a separate room to display new designs and color combinations and work on new projects. Every work week our production schedule included someone's experiment.

New Goals Foster Improvement

Here is an example of how effective new goals such as these can be. Several years ago our first vice president, who was then a kiln supervisor, devised a new way to arrange firing pins on kiln racks that increased the kiln capacity by 20% for each load. Those same racks had been used in the industry for twenty years, and no one had thought to do that before. We pointed out that often it is the new person with a fresh outlook who comes up with the best ideas. For this reason, we gave bonuses to any worker who gave us suggestions for new ideas that improved our company.

Setting goals for each department in the plant fostered a general attitude of anticipation for new ideas and new ways of doing things. Every Monday we awarded bonuses at a general meeting, which also included our office staff. We gave bonuses for new ideas adopted by the company. This generated enthusiasm and a desire to be more observant and look for new and better ways of doing things.

When we arrived at a new technique, a new color, or a new design, we provided samples for our clients. We did this for two reasons: to let them know what was new, in case they could use it, and to let them know we were continually striving for new and better ways to do things. The result was that our customers felt they could rely on us to welcome new and different ideas they might suggest. We tried never to tell a customer "It can't be done." Our goal was to say "We'll try anything." This often resulted in new and unusual techniques and visual effects and ultimately resulted in more sales.

We were a small company, yet our in-house staff included a creative coordinator, a design assistant, and three graphic artists. We used several freelance artists and designers, a well-known hand-painter, and a top designer. We also relied on several consultants in the industry to help us when we needed it.

Market Awareness Generates New Goals

Many ideas are generated by keeping in touch with the general market. We took our key employees to as many association meetings as our work schedule allowed. In addition, throughout the year we visited as many plants, museums, and design facilities as we could, in the United States, in Europe, and in the Orient.

To further expand our awareness of new designs, we subscribed to industry and marketing journals. We also subscribed to as many fine art, museum, and other cultural magazines as we could. We met as many new artists as time and occasion allowed. If we were shopping and discovered a new product or an interesting design or technique, we made a note of it and tried to contact the artist or innovator. The point is, we never stopped thinking about improving our products and modifying our company goals. That contributed to our success.

EMPLOYEES

Sharing Goals with Employees

Another factor that contributed to our success was consistently sharing our goals with our workers. We found that the more we integrate our workers in the total operation of our business, the more concerned they were. On page 76 is an example of the sheet that was in our company handbook. Applicants read it while they were waiting to be interviewed, and our employees were familiar with it because a copy of it was kept in the lunchroom. On the reverse side of the page reproduced on page 76, we included a description of the type of person we wanted to employ (see page 77).

Our workers had a clear idea of who we were, who we needed to work for us, and what we were trying to accomplish. I mentioned the importance of a value system at the beginning of this chapter, and in my book, *People, Common Sense, and the Small Business*. I would like to expand on that subject because I think it is so important for the success of any business.

WHAT WE ARE

We are primarily A MARKETING FIRM. We market, sell and distribute porcelain products.

We are also AN IMPORTING FIRM. We import porcelain products for other companies to market and sell.

We are also A CREATIVE PROJECTS SOURCE. We innovate new ideas for companies who market in the collectibles field.

We are also A SMALL DESIGN STUDIO. We design porcelain products for other companies to produce and sell.

WHAT WE ARE NOT

We are NOT a large manufacturing firm. We don't make any porcelain products here.

We are NOT a plant. We don't operate on a division of labor basis with high production, piece work, conveyors, etc.

WHAT WE DO

We market products that are produced by ourselves and other companies both here and abroad.

We import products that we and other companies market.

We create designs and make the designs into usable form in our graphic arts studio.

We experiment with new designs and new decorating techniques in our studio.

We test our designs by decorating them in our studio.

We innovate decorating procedures other companies can use when they produce our designs.

We solve problems by doing some of the final touches decorating ourselves.

We set the quality standard for other companies who produce our ware.

We test some components and procedures for suppliers and other companies on a limited basis.

WHO WE NEED

A person who is neat, clean (shaven) and well-groomed.

A person who is artistic, or does handicrafts.

A person who has very high standards for themselves.

A person who has good hand-eye coordination.

A person who is patient with repetitive tasks.

A person who is adaptable to changing tasks.

A person who is careful, yet can work efficiently.

A person who has a good attitude toward learning.

A person who can admit and report mistakes.

A person who enjoys a challenge.

A person who wants an opportunity to learn and grow.

Your Value System

Unless your value system supports your goals, you cannot achieve those goals. I knew our company's major goals included a high quality product, fast delivery, and innovative decorating techniques. That meant we had to have supporting goals such as a clean work environment, good customer relations, and a superior work force. That meant we had to hire and train good workers. It also meant we had to have a value system that strengthened those supporting goals.

Our value system included a positive attitude and the belief that it is necessary to admit mistakes in order to learn and grow. Marilyn vos Savant says in her book, *Brain Building*, that the basis for learning is being able to recognize mistakes. You cannot learn if you don't know when you have made an error. Professional athletes, actors, and musicians all learn from their errors. But you have to admit them first to learn from them. That's common sense.

Our American value system does not foster a good learning environment because we are taught from early childhood not to admit or report mistakes. American society teaches that we are not responsible for our neighbors' acts. We punish people who "blow the whistle" or "squeal on others." This attitude carries over to the workplace where workers feel no responsibility to report what goes on around them and leads to workers ignoring, hiding, or denying mistakes. The result is poor quality workmanship.

Establishing Policies that Integrate Workers

To improve the quality of workmanship, you need to change this attitude toward admitting and reporting mistakes. We did that by establishing several policies we consistently enforced. They will work for you too.

The most important thing we did was view mistakes as a natural part of the learning process. This set the tone. Instead of viewing mistakes as some deliberate act meant to hurt the company, or some behavior deserving of punishment, we viewed them as accidents that happen and can be prevented with more experience and care. We freely admitted our own mistakes. We praised others for admitting their mistakes. We never ridiculed workers for making mistakes. We gave bonuses to workers who reported mistakes and awarded those bonuses at weekly awards meetings.

If a worker from any department found a defective plate that was ready to be shipped and reported it, the worker was praised and received a bonus. Our attitude toward mistakes fostered an outlook that was conducive to learning, growing, and producing a high quality product.

By sharing our goals and making the workers an integral part of those goals, we had their full cooperation to help us meet all our goals. It was especially important for our sales service, shipping, and accounting departments to be aware of our goals. These departments were linked directly to our customers. The more informed they were about our basic goals, the more sensitive they were about the roles they played in our success. The degree to which each of our employees shared our goals is epitomized by a card our bookkeeper bought for her desk. When I discovered it one day, she said it reminded her of the need to make collection calls. It read, "A sale is not a sale until the money's in the bank."

When we didn't meet our goals, we shared that with employees too. We also shared financial information with them. We did not confuse them with the accountant's P&L statement. Instead, we kept them apprised of the company's finances with a quarterly financial report so they knew how we were doing. We wanted them to know how important they were for the success of the company.

Helping Employees with Their Goals

We didn't stop there. We had each one of our employees set yearly goals for himself or herself. It was important that they set their own goals and measure their own progress with the company. That way, they knew they were in control of their future.

We kept an open door policy and treated our workers individually, so they knew they could speak for themselves. I found they were always more critical of themselves than we would have been of them.

When we sent supervisors or other employees to seminars or training sessions, they knew our goal was to help them learn and grow in the business. They also knew they had a goal—to share what they learned with others. We pointed out that you learn more when you teach others what you have just discovered. Our approach taught our employees that setting personal goals improves both your attitude and your performance.

Make your workers a part of your team from the beginning. That is easy to do when you have a small business. Share your goals with them. Make certain they understand what you are trying to do. You will find they will be more interested in their jobs and how those jobs contribute to your overall plans. You will find your goals become part of their goals. Helping your employees meet their goals should be one of your major goals.

CUSTOMERS

Keeping Focused on the Customer's Needs

Every successful small business owner knows that three important goals are: knowing who your customer is, supplying what your customer wants, and keeping focused on that customer. Your customer base can change with a changing economy. Be alert to changes and periodically ask yourself who your customer is. What are your goals as they relate to that customer? Where are you going, and why? And how are you going to get there?

Often circumstances beyond your control dictate when you have to change directions or add another direction. Two years after we added our decorating facility, our direct sales customers were declining and the collectibles field, while still a viable market, was becoming increasingly competitive because other decorating plants were entering the field. Gene saw opportunities to fit into a small niche in the collectibles market others couldn't fit. As an opportunist, he saw a need for someone to supply collectibles customers with ideas for projects that included innovative decorating techniques.

Gene is very creative and he knew he could come up with ideas. He also knew I could contribute ideas because several of my jobs in New York had been to create projects for direct sales companies and design jewelry for manufacturers. We knew how to reach other creative people and how to use their talents and services on a consulting basis. Gene had maintained a network of artists and designers established during the years he had spent in the industry.

While Gene was still working for the large china company, he and I often wrote the pattern stories for new designs for his line. He also used a professional writer in New York. One day our daughter Linda told us about a friend who was in her creative writing class in college. We saw some of her friend's work, and Gene immediately hired her on a freelance basis to write pattern stories for him.

Later when we started our small business we hired her as a creative coordinator. She did an excellent job researching projects, writing romantic copy for patterns, writing concepts and stories for collectibles projects, and writing marketing copy for us. When we sold our business, she joined a collectibles company near Philadelphia. She is one of the most gifted copywriters we know. Remember to look around you for talent you can use in your small business.

Even though you have access to established experts in your field, don't overlook opportunities to utilize the talents of people you know. As a small business owner, you have an opportunity to give others experience early in their careers. Sometimes they will stay with you. Sometimes they will move on to bigger companies. Be glad when you can find and use these talented people, even for a short time. Learn from the experience we had with our daughter's friend.

With all our talent for generating ideas, Gene's reason for adding the goal of supplying ideas to others made sense. If we only *decorated* for a company, we were competing with other decorators who could quote lower prices. Gene reasoned that our company would be assured of slightly higher prices and consistent decorating contracts if we generated ideas for projects in exchange for being assured that the companies who used our ideas would also use us as the decorator for those projects.

We soon began selling ideas for collector plates to collectibles companies. This, along with the new decorating techniques we came up with, was an innovative marketing procedure that was quite successful for us.

New Market Niches Bring New Customers

Always be alert and looking for new market niches as customer goals. We focused on a small niche in another market, the upscale custom segment of the restaurant field. Gene had observed there was less competition there. Few companies could maintain the quality standards those customers demanded. Others could not meet the delivery dates they needed. Others who could meet both criteria did not think the individual orders were large enough to bother with.

This market was right for us because we were small, and we could meet the high quality standards and give fast delivery. We created special designs for each restaurant, using a special back-stamp on each item which included the restaurant's name.

This market was composed of expensive dining rooms, private clubs, and affluent individuals. While this may appear to be a mixture of different customers, it was really the same type of customer — a discriminating client who needed high quality china, in small quantities, most often in a hurry, and who was willing to pay for it. We were still following our basic goal of providing a high quality product. We were also focusing on innovative decorating techniques to help us reach our goals. And we maintained our other supporting goals, such as meticulous house-keeping, accurate record-keeping, and high quality performance in customer relations. Our value system was compatible and helped us do these things.

One of our first customers in the new venture of selling to selective clients was the King of Saudi Arabia. The order came through the direct sales network Gene had maintained over the years. When one of Gene's sales contacts had an opportunity to sell china to the King of Saudi Arabia for his private jet and ten airports, he asked us to supply the china. We also supplied the crystal. It was one of our largest orders. More about this in a later chapter.

One of our first customers in the other venture of supplying ideas for collectibles projects was a direct mail company. Gene had the idea to combine metal with porcelain to create a new type of collector plate. We first experimented with the decorating technique to be sure we could produce it. He sold the direct mail company the idea and their staff created a story that lent itself to the product. We decorated a half million plates for them. Soon other companies copied the idea. Now they can be seen in many gift shops in many price ranges.

Selling Your Marketing Rights

When you sell ideas for product development, be careful what you are selling. You need to have either a sound verbal agreement or a written contract to stipulate the marketing rights that you are retaining.

Gene developed another source of revenue by selling the direct mail rights to companies for projects we created while retaining the retail marketing rights ourselves. We did this with our collection of presidential china. We reproduced china patterns of former presidents. Other companies had done this years before. One company produced them as dinner plates, and another company produced them as dessert plates. We decided to issue the china patterns as dessert plates. I suggested we add favorite dessert recipes appropriate for each president as a selling device. Our creative coordinator researched the project and wrote the stories that accompanied each plate. It was a huge success.

We sold the idea to a direct mail collectibles company. By retaining retail rights, we were able to sell the plates to the Presidential Libraries, the Smithsonian, other museums, and better retail stores and catalogs. The plates are still a good item for the company. I styled matching cups and saucers, dinner bells, and porcelain boxes, and suggested other items for the line, while consulting for our company after we retired.

A Good Staff Meets Customers' Goals

We created a number of projects for collectibles companies. We were lucky to have access to good artists and to have a good creative writer on our staff who researched the projects for us. The more creative people you can add to your staff, either as full-time employees or freelance agents, the better off you will be.

If there are certain skills your employees must have to meet customer goals, never stop looking for people with those skills. We needed artistic people who could design, so we were constantly searching for new artists. One of my duties, and the duty of the creative writer, was to be constantly on the lookout for more artists. Even the supervisor of our decal-making department attended quarterly reviews at the art schools nearby to look for artists.

We never pursued licensing, but that is another good marketing aid if you are in the right business. The company our creative coordinator joined is a licensing company.

If your business requires a certain expertise, never become complacent and feel you have satisfied that need permanently with your current staff. You need to be looking constantly. People move away, get married, or just quit work. Whatever expertise you need, be aware of your continuous need for it and never stop looking. Keeping good employees must be one of your major goals. Keeping good suppliers is another of your major goals. To do that, you need to share your goals with them.

SUPPLIERS HERE AND ABROAD

Suppliers are so important for the success of a small business, I want to discuss them again in more detail to illustrate the importance of sharing goals with them. It helps maintain good relations and ultimately contributes to their success as your supplier.

It is easy to deal with suppliers in your own country. You speak the same language, enjoy the same culture, and share the same nationality. Your suppliers understand and respond to the idioms you use in describing what you want. Your ability to communicate is enhanced when you share the same language. It also helps when you share the same culture and the same dialect.

Communicating with Suppliers

Since many small businesses today rely on suppliers from overseas, I want to discuss the techniques we used when dealing with them. Generally, we dealt with them the same way we did with all our suppliers. We established certain modes of behavior that made our job easier and contributed to our success. Other small business owners we know have used many of the same techniques, and these techniques can probably help you too.

We made sure our suppliers knew our major goals and how they contributed to them. We also asked about their goals and how we related to them. We did this by showing them our company catalog and manual that included our promotion pieces and our employee goals. We made a point of periodically visiting our suppliers, having lunch or dinner with them, and making sure they visited our facilities. We did this once a year, even with suppliers abroad, and sometimes more often if there were problems to solve. These were working visits, and we maintained a certain protocol.

When suppliers visited our company, we always bought their meals. When we visited them, they bought the meals, although we offered to. We remembered them with Christmas cards, but we were careful to let them know we neither gave nor accepted gifts. We also made certain they knew our employees never accepted gifts from suppliers.

When we, or any of our staff, telephoned suppliers, we were courteous. When they called us for information, we gave the information in a timely fashion. If we found they did not have our same standards and did not get back to us in time, we continued to call them, or sent them faxes, until we got a response. We were never rude. We found our persistence was enough to motivate them.

When we explained our goals to them, we tried to emphasize

how they contributed to our goals with their particular product or service. If we had any problems with their product, we told them quickly. We were just as quick to compliment them. If they had questions about any of our goals, we answered them as succinctly as possible. While we didn't give them trade secrets, we were as open and honest with them as we could be. They knew we expected the same courtesy.

Talking frequently with our suppliers, we learned their goals and their quality standards. If we found a supplier could not, or would not, meet our quality standards, we found another supplier, severing the relationship amicably.

Visiting Suppliers

We visited our suppliers at least once a year, and more frequently if there was any trouble. We also sent our supervisors, sales service people, and managers to visit domestic suppliers at different times during their training. We did this to help improve our performance, believing that the more our employees knew about each segment of the business, the better equipped they were to do their jobs. Our people shared what they learned when they returned, and all of us benefited from their trips.

Although we sent our people to visit suppliers for the reasons I have described, we discovered it was a good way to impress our suppliers. They realized we cared about our people and about maintaining high standards. It contributed to our good relationship with suppliers and accounted for the extra effort they gave when we needed it most.

When we attended our suppliers' trade shows or industry association meetings, we were friendly, and went to cocktail parties and dinners sponsored by our suppliers. However, we never socialized with any of them other than during business dinners or meetings. We maintained a friendly, businesslike relationship.

No matter what factory we visited, we observed the production flow, the storage arrangements, and the labor force. While Gene discussed his business, I talked with the managers about personnel policies and took pictures everywhere we went. If you use these techniques, always ask permission and never photograph anything that might be perceived as proprietary or experimental.

We borrowed some of our decorating ideas from other suppliers here and abroad. We also borrowed ideas for better storage methods. We profited so much from our suppliers and our competition that I wrote a keynote speech and article titled, "Competition, A Challenge For Success," describing all the things we learned from competitors and suppliers here and abroad.

We found the more interest you show in others, the more

interest they show in you, and the more eager they are to help you. Never worry about telling others something that might help them. Instead, share what you can with others. You will find that it is in mutual sharing that both companies are enriched. We found everyone was helpful because they knew we were interested in what they were doing and how they were doing it.

I mentioned earlier that we often took side trips to see sites of interest when traveling. We found that suppliers are eager to suggest places and often take you. Even though we insisted on paying, oftentimes they would take us as guests. Most of the time, except when visiting Japan, we preferred to strike out on our own, with only our suppliers' suggestions to guide us.

Checking Suppliers' Quality

Our favorite method of checking items being produced for us by our suppliers had two parts. We checked the items during production and then visited the shipping area and asked to see cartons that had been packed for shipment. We had the cartons opened and went through them with the managers and inspectors. Even though we didn't speak their language in some cases, if we were overseas, we gestured and shook our heads to indicate which pieces were acceptable and which were not.

Courtesy Letters

After visiting any plant here or abroad, I always sent thank-you notes when we returned. If we had borrowed a technique or a storage arrangement from them, I made sure to send a picture of the improvement that came as a result of their suggestions. Sometimes I just described the changes. If we had taken side trips to see their area, I always described what we saw and how much we enjoyed our stay. I considered these personal thank-you notes important. In addition, Gene sent formal business letters after our visits.

You may feel formal business letters are adequate after you have visited suppliers here and abroad. If you are traveling alone, or with a business associate, such formal thank-you notes are just fine. If you are a husband and wife team as we were, and you express a personal interest in them, I believe you create a better image. We found extending additional courtesies to them resulted in their extending the same courtesies to us.

Suppliers Overseas

If your business takes you to Europe or England, you will have little difficulty communicating. It was easiest working with the British because we share the same language. However, the dialect is different so we had to be conscious of idioms that might be confusing when discussing details. This was especially necessary when discussing weights and measures.

A number of small businesses are either exporting to Japan or importing Japanese products. If any of your suppliers are Japanese you may want to buy Mitchell Deutsch's book, *Doing Business With the Japanese* (New American Library, 1985) or *Doing Business in Asia* by David L. James (Betterway Books, 1993). Since we worked with the Japanese for a number of years, I will give you a brief description of experiences that may be helpful to you if you travel to the Orient.

You may find it difficult to communicate and somewhat of a culture shock to do business in the Orient. It is easier to do business there or in any country if your suppliers or one of their key people speaks English. Most of them do. If they do not, you will need a reliable interpreter. Be sure you get one from your industry, because when you return home you will find yourselves sending faxes back and forth and making phone calls.

You will have no problem with the exchange rate. You can use small calculators. You will, however, have a slight problem with the great time change when you travel to the Orient. There is a twelve- or thirteen-hour time change between Japan and New York. Eight in the morning in New York is eight or nine in the evening in Tokyo, depending on daylight saving time. The travel time is more than double that of traveling across the United States or traveling from New York to London. You need to keep that time change in mind when you are dealing by fax and telephone.

Jet lag takes a toll, and if you are trying to make every dollar count while you are overseas you want to work as long hours as you can while you are there. I suggest you eat lightly on the plane, drink plenty of liquids (no alcohol), and try not to sleep too much. By the time you arrive in Japan, you may be alert enough to do some business, but I recommend you try to get at least one night's sleep before you begin working.

Never take more luggage than you can carry. Do not wear laced shoes because you will be slipping out of your shoes at many offices and factories in Japan. Women will be more comfortable in full skirts or slacks, because you will be sitting on the floor cross-legged like the men some of the time.

Working with the Japanese

We worked with the Japanese for fourteen years and enjoyed it. They work long hours just as American small business owners do. They are courteous, punctual, and eager to please. Suppliers generally meet you at your hotel and take you directly to their showrooms or factories. In many cases, be prepared for long automobile rides because factories are often located in outlying regions. If showrooms are in a large city, traffic will account for the long, tiring trips. When you arrive at their office, Japanese serve visitors a small cup of tea before doing business. Sip it. If you drink every cup, by the time you visit several showrooms or factories, you will be waterlogged and waste too much time going to the bathroom.

Your overseas suppliers work at the pace you set. If you give the impression you want to sleep late, work short hours, and party, they will comply. If they know you are there to work hard and learn much, they will accommodate you. In our case, they knew we represented a small American business, we wanted to work long hours, and we tried to accomplish as much as possible in as short a time as possible. We worked longer hours day in and day out in Japan than anywhere else in the world. We decided on our first trip that they were the only suppliers who could maintain our pace indefinitely.

We made it clear from the beginning what our goals were, how high our standards were, and what our future plans were. Thus, our work day began at seven or eight in the morning and ended at nine or ten in the evening. We worked all day Saturday and Sunday. We ate a box lunch at the factories or went with their managers to a nearby restaurant.

While some of the lunches were rushed because we were trying to accomplish as much as possible during the day, the evening meals were more relaxed and quite enjoyable. During these leisure hours, you will establish informal networks that affect your formal relationship with the Japanese. Because we were a husband and wife team, they invited us to their homes after several years of doing business with them. We were honored. When they visited the United States, we invited them to our home.

The Japanese were the only suppliers with whom we exchanged gifts. We did this because they initiated it and it is their custom. Like suppliers everywhere, they appreciate your willingness to learn about their culture and their cuisine. If you stay at Japanese hotels in provincial areas and eat the traditional food, you will have fish, miso soup, rice, and salad for breakfast, gray or green noodles with broth for lunch, and many courses of fish, seafood, vegetables, and tofu for dinner, but no sweet desserts. In Korea, Taiwan, Hong Kong, and Thailand, more sweets are served. Gene always missed American pastries when we traveled in Japan. I missed peanut butter.

Learning from the Japanese

The Japanese are courteous, careful, and the cleanest people we have met. They even wear gauze masks when they have colds to prevent infecting others. If you follow their customs, you will wash your hands with a damp cloth before touching food, and remove your shoes and don slippers before entering a house, a restaurant, or an office. You will remove slippers before entering a dining room, and you will put on different slippers before entering the bathroom.

The Japanese set such a good example with their clean, well-organized factories that you will want to borrow from them. We did. We modeled our housekeeping procedures after them (without the slipper routine, of course). We also borrowed our arrangement of space from them and certain production techniques.

Rather than ask the Japanese to lower their standards and slow down so we could compete, as one major American car manufacturer has done, we told our people about the Japanese quality and their high production quotas.

We found competing with the Japanese improved our performance. It also established good relations with them. They have a high regard for Americans and feel complimented when Americans borrow ideas or production methods from them.

In the years we did business with the Japanese, we worked long, productive hours. We dealt with small companies and large ones. Their eagerness to please and willingness to work were refreshing. We began working with them out of necessity, when our American suppliers couldn't keep pace with Gene's production needs. They put the customer first and directed all their goals to meeting our production needs.

Over the years, we have noticed changes due to a gradual westernization. When we first began going there, we heard little or no English on the streets, in hotels, or on television. With each successive trip, we notice more Americans in hotels, stores, and factories and more English spoken in those places.

Our perception of all the countries to which we traveled is colored by the places we visited to conduct our business. We saw only the towns that fostered the ceramic industry. In England it was Stoke-on-Trent; in Japan it was Nagoya, Mizunami, Seto, and Tajimi; in Taiwan, Taipei; in Thailand, Bangkok; in Korea, Seoul; and in all of them the nearby regions.

Clarifying Notions about Overseas Suppliers

There are a few notions about the Japanese and other Oriental overseas suppliers that will help you if you do business with them. The first concerns pricing. Items sent to the United States go through very limited profit levels from manufacturer to consumer. In Japan they go through five or more profit levels from manufacturer to consumer. Consequently, Japanese items exported to the United States generally can be purchased cheaper here than in Japan. In other Oriental countries, they may not have as many profit levels as Japan but often more than we have.

Another notion concerns quality. Be aware that you need to check items as carefully with Japanese suppliers as with any other supplier, especially if there is much hand labor involved. We have discovered there is variation in handmade items produced by the same supplier. You will find it necessary to continually check the quality of pieces being produced by different companies to ensure consistency. Once your overseas suppliers know the quality standard they have to meet, they will meet it. When they know the delivery dates they must meet, they will generally meet them.

One misconception about the Japanese and other overseas suppliers is that one huge factory produces everything that it sells. If you use overseas suppliers, be aware that in many cases they subcontract some or all of their work. It is disconcerting to American business people to learn that the ware they purchase from one factory is actually made in several different factories. If you want to check on their production techniques and quality control, you need to visit each of the smaller factories that supply the large factory from which you are buying.

In the Japanese ceramic industry, cups may be made in one plant and saucers in another. In Japan, Taiwan, and Korea, smaller companies, such as the figurine plants we visited, may use several families to sculpt, paint, and produce ware in their homes. The ware is then sold to a large plant that markets it as their ware. Recently, the Japanese and Koreans have been subcontracting their work to factories in other countries. They are also building plants in third world countries, the United States, and Europe.

Summing Up Overseas Suppliers

When we visited our overseas suppliers, some of them had hung pictures of my magazine articles in their showrooms. They were proud to be associated with us and eager to show us that they had read the articles. We found it helped emphasize our goals and helped promote us overseas with our suppliers and with other companies who visited them.

If you do business with suppliers overseas, you will want them to visit your company to establish good relations. We wanted our overseas suppliers to see how clean our work environment was and how it contributed to our major goal of a high quality product. We wanted to show them how their high standards had helped us meet our goals. We also wanted them to see the latest things we were working on. We felt the more they knew about us, the more dedicated they would be to helping us meet our goals.

We established such good relations with our overseas suppliers that it was difficult to break the ties after we sold our business. Although we dealt with suppliers from several different countries, only the Japanese suppliers called us after we retired. If they became confused about something under the new management, they would ask us to explain it in more detail. Although we referred their calls to our former company's office, Gene also spent time with them by phone putting them at ease and making sure they still had confidence in our company and understood its goals. It was difficult to break ties after fourteen years.

We still communicate with a few of our suppliers. We exchange Christmas cards, family pictures, and newsy letters. We consider them more than business acquaintances now. We value them as friends.

You may use different methods to communicate with your suppliers and different techniques to inspect their ware, establish quality standards, and delivery schedules. The ones I have described worked for us and have worked for other small businesses who use overseas suppliers. The major criterion is to maintain a friendly business relationship. Let them know your standards by your behavior and they won't disappoint you.

Get the best suppliers here and abroad and share your goals with them. Let them know the important role they play in helping you meet your goals. It will improve your chances for success as a small business.

4.

Promoting Your Business

To have a successful business, you need to promote it. Promoting your business means talking about it to everyone you know. It means finding ways to let customers, and potential customers, know about your product and your company. The more people who know about you, the more likely you are to succeed.

Recognition and Awards

Local and Regional Recognition

There are a number of ways to promote your small business without spending too much money. If your customers reside in your community, find ways to make your company's name well known. Support local sports teams, clubs, and other organizations. Sponsor local contests or community projects, such as marathons and 4-H activities. The positive publicity you receive helps you expand your customer base and helps you recruit workers. When we first started our company, we sponsored a baseball team and a 4-H project. We did this even though our customers did not reside in our community because we knew it would give us a good reputation in the community and bring us some good workers.

Excel in whatever you do, and you will qualify for awards from regional and state agencies. This is an excellent way to promote your business as a quality organization. Awards give you something to talk about with your customers and help motivate your employees.

We received two regional awards for energy conservation. Two activities brought it about. We used an energy-saving device to recycle the heat our kilns generated, and we used an overlapping schedule to fire our kilns. As a result, we saved thousands of dollars in electricity each year and provided a better environment for our workers.

James Dunlevy (left), Pennsylvania Power Co. Vice President, presents awards to Pat and Gene Tway of Woodmere Inc. This photo and a short article appeared in the *New Castle News* and other regional papers on February 8, 1984. We received the first Pennsylvania Power Company Load Management Award, which recognizes successful results by customers in the use of electricity during Penn Power's "off-peak" hours. We also received Penn Power's Optimum Energy Citation, honoring design excellence in overall thermal efficiency and use of energy-efficient equipment based on the actual amount of electricity used in a year.

We used the awards to show our customers we were saving them money by conserving on fuel consumption during production. The awards let everyone know we were a progressive company looking for new and more efficient ways to produce our china. It also motivated our employees because they knew we were providing the best environment we could.

Industry Awards and National Contests

Industry awards are another way to promote your company. These awards are important because they bring you recognition throughout your industry and may get you more business. Our good reputation, due to industry awards, helped us get decorating jobs from friendly competitors. A few of the largest and best china producers in America asked us to decorate for them several different times when they needed additional production.

This is the George O'Brien collection of giftware that received numerous awards. George O'Brien, formerly Vice President of Design at Tiffany's, a designer who worked with us, won the Discovery Award from the Society of Glass and Ceramic Decorators for his elephant teapot. A feature story about the design and our company appeared in *Gifts & Decorative Accessories* magazine, April 1984. Photo courtesy Edward Lawrence Studio.

Industry seminars promote your business too. You meet new people, learn about new products and new production techniques that will help promote your business. When we attended our first association meeting, we met a number of color suppliers who were featuring their latest products. I noticed some unusual new colors and asked for several samples.

We conducted a number of tests using the colors. The result was a new look and a new decorating technique. As soon as we had some plates decorated with designs that used the new technique, we knew we had a winner. Gene showed the samples to one of our customers who liked it and thought it would make an unusual border for a collector plate series, which they then created.

Enter as many national contests as you can. When you enter contests, you have to supply photographs of your product. The cost of the photographs is more than offset by the publicity and national recognition you receive. The more national recognition you receive, the more credibility you have. It also motivates your sales reps in different regions of the country.

Awards like these bring you publicity far in excess of what you could afford. We were on magazine covers four times, three for awards we received and one for a cover story I wrote.

This photo appeared on the cover of *Ceramic Bulletin*, October 1985. I wrote an article in that issue about our innovative decorating techniques. Courtesy of *Ceramic Bulletin*.

This photo was used on the cover of *Restaurant Hospitality* magazine, November 1988. It featured the winners of the 23rd Annual Table Top Awards. Our award-winning custom china design for Carmel Valley resort was selected for the cover. Reprinted with permission from *Restaurant Hospitality* magazine, Nov. 1988 issue, © 1988, Penton Publishing Inc.

This is a service plate of the china I designed for President Jimmy Carter's fly-fishing cabin in Eljay, GA. A photo of the china appeared in The Living Arts section of *The New York Times*, March 23, 1990. The day the article appeared, our company received dozens of phone calls from people who wanted to order similar sets. Photo courtesy Edward Lawrence Studio.

Important Customers Bring Recognition

Sell your products to prestigious clients and you gain recognition through your association with them. Customers like to do business with companies that sell to important people. It validates their judgment selecting you as a company.

We were lucky the King of Saudi Arabia was one of our first important customers. Gene used other networks to get clients. One contact helped us supply a china service for President and Mrs. Jimmy Carter. Another contact, interior designer Carleton Varney, helped us supply the official service for the Vice President's House in Washington DC. Neither china service was purchased with taxpayers' money; both were donated.

Your reps may lead you to prestigious customers. When they do, give the order the attention it deserves. One of our reps from the hotel division got us several orders with influential people who wanted to design their own china and have it produced exclusively for themselves. Orders like this are generally small and costly to produce. We found the large companies who were our competitors were generally approached first by these people because of their high profile. The large companies normally turned

I designed this china with Carleton Varney for the vice president's mansion in Washington, DC. Woodmere produced the official china service for fifty. This photo appeared in the Home Front section of *The Washington Post*, November 14, 1991. The pattern has a light blue marbleized border with a gold line on the outer rim and inner border. The vice presidential seal is featured in gold at the center of the plate and is highlighted with a soft pink starburst. Photo courtesy Edward Lawrence Studio.

them down because the orders weren't large enough and were too time consuming.

We took any size order if the price was right. Sometimes this led us into projects involving new decorating techniques or unusual delivery service. One client needed a complete service of china for twenty-four people within two weeks. That was the fastest order we ever produced. If one of your goals is supplying important clients, be prepared to do whatever is necessary to meet that goal.

Your willingness to do the unusual to promote your business may lead you to unexpected windfalls. For example, I mentioned earlier the order for the King of Saudi Arabia. This began with a phone call from one of Gene's contacts asking if we would be willing to work on a custom order for the King. The initial order of $25,000 was so small the larger, more prestigious companies didn't want to be bothered because it would require a great deal of time and effort.

Gene saw a promotional value in an order coming from a King, although it was actually coming from Boeing. The china was to be used in the private jet they were building for the King. We worked on the samples for several months and got Boeing to add a number of additional china items. At this point, the potential order had grown to approximately $70,000, a really large amount for our small company.

We produced the samples, made a final presentation, and waited several months for their decision. When we received the order, it was eleven times the size of the initial order because the King flew into ten different ground locations around the world and needed a service for each. The final order totaled more than $750,000. Our willingness to work on a small order helped promote our company far beyond what we could have imagined.

Other ways to promote your business are through: (1) your banker and investors, (2) your business plan, (3) advertising, (4) public relations, and (5) trade shows.

BANKERS AND INVESTORS

Have you ever promoted your business with your banker? Few small business owners take the time or trouble. We did, and consider it one of the reasons for our success. We believe the money you get from banks is in proportion to the trust they have in you. Your job as a small business owner is to sell your business and yourself to people who can lend you money.

As long as you are in business and growing, you will need to borrow money. It is more difficult to get money in the early stages when you don't have a track record. That is why you need to promote your business from the start. After you have established your credibility, you will find bankers and investors are more receptive to your requests for loans.

Viewing Your Banker as a Business Partner

You should view your banker almost as a business partner. Select a senior member of the bank to visit each time you go, and establish a good relationship. This will help you maintain a high profile at the bank. Gene selected the senior vice president to visit each time and considered him an integral part of our team. When people told us how much they envied us because we didn't have a boss, we were quick to remind them that we did have one—the bank.

Initiate conferences with your banker, arrive promptly, and bring material that shows what you have accomplished. If you want more money, bring additional paperwork to justify that need. If you have a partner who is responsible for an important segment of your business, bring that person along to answer questions.

Gene scheduled these conferences at our bank on a quarterly basis for the duration we owned the company. There were times when we had more than one conference during a quarter. The purpose for these extra meetings was to lay the groundwork in case we needed more money sooner than we had projected.

Our conferences with the bank actually began before we started our company, while Gene was still working for a large corporation and I was teaching. We visited our banker and told him what we planned to do in the future. Gene asked for suggestions to help us get started. He treated our banker as a respected advisor, made an appointment, and gave a carefully planned sales presentation that was structured to convince the banker we would be good risks as business owners.

Sharing Plans to Establish Trust

Share your marketing plans with your banker, just as you do with your employees, suppliers, and customers. The more you share with the bank, the more credibility you build. Bring the latest news releases, awards, and other PR material about your company. If you have new products, bring pictures along with your company catalog. Also bring current financial statements and provide your banker with a new business plan each year.

Part of promoting your company with the bank is establishing mutual trust. You do this when you share the bad news too. Bankers and investors don't like surprises. Warn them of a problem as early as you can and include the steps you are taking to solve the problem. Don't dwell on why it occurred, emphasize how you are overcoming it. Your veracity, together with your positive attitude, builds integrity with the bank.

You should be as concerned about each meeting at the bank as you are about major sales presentations for your most discriminating customers or your biggest accounts. Never hurriedly grab a bunch of papers and head for the bank, or drop in unannounced, not if the consequences are important to you. The bank should be a major part of your marketing strategy to get what you want. Treat it with the importance it deserves.

One advantage of doing business with a small bank is that they get to know you faster and easier. One disadvantage is the limit they can loan any single customer. A federal regulation limited our bank's ability to loan more than one million dollars to a single customer. In our early days, Gene used irrevocable letters of credit from customers as collateral for loans from our bank.

The federal limit on our bank became a worrisome problem as we grew, and almost forced us to use another bank. Fortunately, before we did, the regulation was changed and our bank expanded, doubling the amount of their loan limit.

Dealing in Foreign Currency

If you do business with other countries and deal in their currency, you may want to buy currency futures to ensure that your buying price is secure. Here's why. If you buy $100,000 in product at a certain cost and the currency relationship fluctuates so that the dollar is worth less, you lose money. If you purchase currency futures, you ensure that the cost of your product will remain the same. You need to work closely with your banker to make certain both you and the banker understand and agree with what you are doing.

We did this because we bought our china blanks from Japan and committed to our purchases six months or more in advance. We purchased in yen rather than dollars. If between the time we placed an order and the time shipment was made the yen/dollar relationship fluctuated (as it generally did), we either lost part or all of our profit or we earned extra profit. We overcame this problem by buying yen futures when we believed we were in a period of a declining dollar. We would commit to enough yen futures to cover six months of purchasing and then roll them into future months if shipments were delayed. These futures protected our profit.

If you are buying components in another currency you should investigate both futures and options. There are advantages and disadvantages to both. If your local bank cannot help you with this, have them introduce you to their correspondent bank that has an international department. While it is a good idea to use your local bank as much as possible, don't limit what you can do by what your local bank knows or can do. When and if the need occurs, promote your business even beyond your local bank.

Visits from Your Banker

Invite your local banker or investors to visit your facility. They will be more comfortable if they know what your company looks like. That is why you must provide an ideal work environment for your employees. It motivates them and gives you the kind of image you need to make a good impression on the bank and other visitors.

We invited the executives from our bank and found they often brought their wives. We encouraged them to bring any other business people they wanted. We did such a good job of promoting our company with the bank that the bank actually helped us promote our business with others. We got a few customers through the visitors the bank executives brought with them.

Investing Back in Your Business

You promote yourself with the bank by how much you are personally willing to invest in your company. When we started our marketing company, we borrowed all we could on our insurance policies and later signed notes for our other assets. We jokingly said we mortgaged everything but the animals and ourselves. Our willingness to put our life savings on the line helped promote us with the bank. Later, after we were successfully operating our business and making good money, we invested our newly earned money back in our business.

Your willingness to put your own money back in the business after you are making good returns also promotes your image with your bank and investors. They are more comfortable knowing you have that much faith in your business and knowing you are not working just to take what you can out of the business before dumping it. The more we invested back in our business, the more it promoted our image with the bank. When you go heavily in debt to start your own business and continue investing your money in it, you had better have a good business plan.

YOUR BUSINESS PLAN

The most important promotion piece you take to the bank or to any investor is your business plan. It ensures your success with them. Someone may know you well and have faith in your abilities to create a product or perform a service, but if you can't express yourself in writing and show that you can plan ahead, even your closest friend or relative will hesitate to invest money in your venture.

What a Business Plan Says and Does

A business plan is not difficult to write if you organize your thoughts. The major purpose of a business plan is to serve as a road map for your company and your people. Your business plan should tell where you are going and how and when you are going to get there. Our plan described these five things: (1) the size and breadth of the market, (2) where we fit in the market, (3) what made our company special, (4) sales and profit goals, and (5) how we planned to get there.

We showed a three-year plan but got a commitment for one year's financing. The further you project, the less accurate your forecast can be. But a three-year projection gives you more credibility and leaves the impression that you plan to be around for a long time.

Your business plan should include a marketing plan, a manufacturing plan, and a financial plan. Integrate these three elements so that they support the overall business plan. Carefully explore and describe each segment. Include promotional material and your catalog or pictures of your product.

Our business plan included three companies: our marketing company, our decal company, and our china decorating company. Gene always combined these into one business plan so it was easier for the bank to understand. Here is an example.

BUSINESS PLAN

Table of Contents
Woodmere China, Inc

Overview—previous year
Marketing Plans—next three years
Color brochures, editorials, news releases
Manufacturing Plans—personnel requirements
Financial Plan—next three years
Inventory/Receivables, Pro Forma statements

The Overview was a description of the company's activities for the previous year. It described what had happened to the company that year and why. Any problem areas were explained, and our plan for solutions was outlined. All our successes were emphasized. The Overview ended with a positive outlook for the future. For example: "All these developments make us feel quite optimistic about the coming year and the years following. This optimism is reflected in the plans that follow."

Marketing, Manufacturing, and Financial Plans

Our marketing plan showed the market size, how our product was different from our competitors', where we fit in the market, and how we were going to penetrate it. Gene tried to be as precise as possible, stating how much business we expected to generate with our plan. He was careful not to overstate our goals.

The color brochures showed our most prestigious products. Later, when we could show published articles, editorials, and press releases about awards we had received, we included those. We brought anything that would make us look progressive.

Our manufacturing plan showed how that operation would be utilized to support the marketing plan. If we had to purchase new equipment we showed how it would be utilized. Personnel requirements included a description of the jobs we needed to increase. We showed how long it would take to hire, train, and develop the people to fill those jobs and meet production goals.

Our financial plan included a financial statement with a balance sheet showing our assets, liabilities, and equity and a profit and loss statement. It also showed how we would arrange financing to support the additional business our marketing plan generated. If you grow too fast and you can't support the inventory and/or receivables, you will lose your customers. Growing too fast without financial backing can put a small business out of business.

Here is an example. We have a friend in the contracting business who sold a three million dollar job for road construction. He didn't plan well enough and didn't realize his finances and credit could not support such a large order. He ultimately lost the order and his business.

Emphasize Your Employees' Skills

Whenever you discuss the management end of your business and how it contributes to your company's overall success, do not overstate the part you play in it. It is a temptation with small business owners to emphasize their personal achievements in the company. This gives the appearance that the owner is indispensable. It tends to make the banker nervous about what would happen if the owner dropped dead tomorrow.

It is much better if you emphasize the skills of your people and their contributions. But be careful that you don't make it sound as if your business hinges on one or two of your key people. You can avoid this if you let your banker know that you cross-train your employees to ensure that all of your people are valuable, yet no one is indispensable.

We were strong believers in cross-training. It provides back-ups for every job and helps prevent layoffs. Everyone in our company knew how to perform several jobs. When business was slow in certain departments, we moved workers to other departments. Several office people could perform important plant jobs, and several plant people could perform important office jobs. We made certain the bank knew about our cross-training and that we had highly skilled, well-trained people. We also made sure they knew no one was indispensable—not even us.

ADVERTISING

Using the Media

You don't need a large advertising budget to succeed in a small business, if you shop carefully and use the media wisely. The standard way to promote your business is by advertising through magazines, television, radio, newspapers, and/or direct mail. At different times, you will want to promote your business through these media. But don't be locked into doing what everyone else does. Instead, select the best method for your business. If you have a unique product or service, and specific customers you must reach, think of unique ways to reach them. If you feel that you can do something different on your own to promote your business, do so.

We did very little advertising with the media because we felt it was not the best way to reach our particular customers with our limited budget. Instead, we spent our money advertising through printed brochures, photographs, catalogs, and some limited mailings we designed specifically to reach our customers. Our approach was so successful I want to share it with you. It may give you ideas for your business.

One special item we created was a Design System that allowed customers in the commercial field to design their own china patterns. It was a series of acrylic overlays of different designs that a person could place over an undecorated plate or photo of a plate. It was a handy device that helped our reps during a sales presentation. Gene had initially developed it while working as a marketing director for another china company. No one there saw its potential, but we did.

Direct Mail

If you rely on direct mail, do some research first. Know your goal. Direct mail can be used to obtain leads or to sell your product. The most important factor in direct mail is the list you use. You can buy lists from brokers. If you buy a list, make certain it is targeted for your market and that you know how old the list is. The older the list, the worse it is. People move, and you may find you have an outdated list that is not worth the mailing cost. When mailing to a new list, the Postal Service will make address corrections for an additional charge. You should mail to a small segment of a mailing list first to check the rate of response before mailing to the entire list. If the rate of response is poor, you save money by not mailing to the entire list and by not buying that list again.

Many mail older companies have found that if you make a second mailing to the same list within thirty days, your mailing may pull 50% or even more of the response of the first mailing. Your mailing should show them how your product benefits them in some way rather than just describing features.

We used direct mailings to obtain leads for our commercial division, and to sell a series of plates for our collectibles market. With the commercial mailing, we found our response rate for getting leads increased with each mailing in the early years. We think this was because our image was growing due to trade shows and to the mailings themselves. We found that giving some basic product knowledge in each mailing helped increase the response. With the collectibles mailing, we found that it was more successful if we accepted credit card orders. We also found you don't make money unless the customer takes several plates in a series.

If you work through an advertising agency for your literature, you will pay an extra 17.5% commission to them. They will do everything, including all copy writing. If you decide to do this yourself, locate the best color printing company in your area and ask them to recommend the best art studio to help you create camera-ready art for the printer. Using the best artists saves you money because the printer doesn't have to charge you for "cleaning up" messy artwork.

Your Company Logo and Catalog

You need a company logo and company color. They should be appropriate for your company and your product or service. Logos become outdated in appearance. When you notice your logo looks a bit old, don't hesitate to have it restyled. Color doesn't get old as fast. The Hershey brown candy wrapper is known the world over and still looks timely.

Our first company logo looked old after the first few years, so we had it restyled. The artist created a single letter, combining stylized versions of our major products. It was so well done, it still looks fresh and exciting ten years later. Our company color, a rich shade of blue, still looks good. We used that color for everything: our catalog cover, our trade booth, the logo on our stationery, business cards, and office supplies. Industry people and customers began to associate our company with that shade of blue. We never changed the color in the fourteen years we owned the business.

We believe one reason for our success was our catalog. Before you create your catalog study the competition. You can learn a great deal from them. Observe what successful companies are doing. Study as many catalogs as you can to see what it is you do or don't like. You will notice that big companies with large advertising budgets have bound catalogs. They can afford the luxury of discarding catalogs each time they add a few new pages. Small companies can't afford to do that.

After studying the competition, Gene decided to use a three-ring notebook for several reasons. We wanted our catalog to sell the total concept of our company to everyone who saw it—the supplier, sales rep, customer, employee, and banker. We also wanted our catalog to show individuals the total range of what we could do, within our specialized market, and we wanted our catalog to show new items in a timely fashion. With a three-ring notebook you can do all these things. Just remove the outdated sheets and insert the new ones. Be sure your books stay clean. You make a bad impression if any of the pages look dog-eared.

Our notebook was a total presentation of all our products to show our decorating capacity. Our book presented commercial, retail, commemorative, and premium incentive china, collectibles, and blank ware. In the back of the book, we included press releases, awards, and other photographs that showed what we had done that was worthy of recognition. We identified different segments of the book with pages that had extended tabs, so readers could quickly find the pages of special interest to them. The notebook was a powerful selling tool and helped promote our business with everyone who saw it.

Using Photographs

Whether or not you have a catalog, whenever you have your products photographed for advertising copy use some of your other products (if you have them) as props for the featured items. Also have items that have been photographed separately printed on one sheet if the items relate to a single concept. For example, in our case if a collector plate series was composed of twelve plates we had all twelve photographs combined on one sheet.

If we had a series of plates in the commercial division that related to an idea we were promoting, we had them photographed separately but printed together. We found it was less expensive, yet made a more impressive statement. For example, when we promoted service plates—those oversized plates that are placed on tables at fine restaurants before you eat—we had them photographed separately because each required special lighting, but we combined the separate photographs on one layout. We chose the ones we had produced for famous or expensive restaurants, or plates that were particularly unusual.

This served two purposes: it showed the customer that we had produced plates for impressive customers, and it showed different types of service plates that we could produce for them. No two service plates were the same, but the basic concepts were

I designed this pattern, Pianissimo, for the Youngstown Symphony Society. It was used in their silent auction during a fund-raising campaign. It was so successful, we added it to our regular line and it became one of our most popular patterns. Photo by Edward Lawrence Studio.

similar and were adaptable for different types of restaurants. There is an example on page 108.

When you are creating catalog pages to show your product, you may not have to use color. Sometimes black and white line drawings can be effective. We used one color silhouettes on white paper to illustrate shapes of items in our line. We also used black and white photographs to illustrate our undecorated china. Sometimes we used blue ink with white paper, since blue was our company's color.

Here is another example of the silhouette type of artwork that can give detailed examples of your product without costing you too much money.

Shop Wisely and Get the Best

One final suggestion: don't skimp or cut corners with your advertising budget. We used the finest components and best artists for our design system, our color brochures, stationery, business cards, and office supplies. You need not be extravagant. Shop wisely, get several quotes before giving an order, and constantly check competitive prices. Here is an example of what we did to get the best discounts on office supplies.

Shortly after we started our business, we established credit with a local office supplier who gave us a good discount. For the duration we owned our business, we bought our furniture and most of our office supplies from him. Yet he knew that whenever mail order catalog houses sent us discount prices I would check them against his prices. If the mail order catalog prices were cheaper and the quality was the same, I notified our local office supplier. I wanted him to have the opportunity to meet their prices rather than switch suppliers. He always met the cheaper prices for us.

PUBLIC RELATIONS

Public relations is another way to promote your small business and make it successful. We relied a great deal on public relations to promote our business because we believed our dollars would go further. You can work as your own public relations director or hire someone as we did.

The Public Relations Director

One way to get a good public relations director is through trade associations. We met our public relations director at one of those meetings. She did such a good job of promoting the association and helping small companies like ours learn more about public relations that we decided to hire her rather than use the "how to" PR kit she had assembled for the association members to use.

Select your PR company based on what they can do for you and on your ability to communicate with them. Don't base your decision on their location. Our PR person was in Chicago and our company was near Pittsburgh. You are as close as a telephone and fax machine. If you do it right, your PR director will get you into magazines, trade journals, newsletters, and trade show papers by working through the editorial departments, not the advertising sections.

You can utilize the PR director in several ways. First, if you have any new production technique, new service, or new personnel or promotions, tell your PR director. You may not see anything exciting about it but a good PR person will. He or she will contact all of the trade magazines and newspapers by telephone and follow up with press releases. Every time we won an award, our PR director sent releases to major industry magazines.

Set the Mood with

Service Plates

There's no second chance at first impressions. A custom designed service plate immediately tells customers they have chosen to dine where quality is imperative. Woodmere works with existing art and colors to match any logo and decor, or an in-house art staff can create art. Let Woodmere show you how to pair a custom service plate with any of their Award Collection dinnerware patterns or carry out the new design for an entire custom tabletop look.

Woodmere's Service Plates.

The Seafood Collection

The Awards Collection

WOODMERE CHINA

Woodmere has a full range of dinnerware and accessory items, all available in the pattern of your choice. Because each piece is fully vitrified with a brilliant hard glaze the look will last and last.

12" Rim Plate
10¾" Rim Plate
10¼" Rim Plate
9¼" Rim Plate
8¼" Rim Plate
7½" Rim Plate
6½" Rim Plate
4" Rim Plate

Octagonal Rim Plate
10¾"

Can Cup
8 oz.

Can Saucer
6" dia.

Can A.D. Cup
3½ oz.

Can A.D. Saucer
4" dia.

Tall Cup
8 oz.

Standard Saucer
6" dia.

Mug
8 oz. & 10 oz.

Ovide Cup
8 oz.

Butter Tub
3 oz.
1⅝" high
3" dia.

Sauceboat
6 oz.

Ice Cream/Sherbert
10 oz.

8½" Oval Platter
14" Oval Platter
12" Oval Platter

Two-Handled Cream Soup
4½" dia., 10 oz.

Bouillon
3¾" dia., 8 oz.

Cream Soup Saucer
6½" dia.

Rim Soup
9¼" dia., 14 oz.
8¼" dia., 12 oz.

Grapefruit/Cereal
7½" dia., 8 oz.

Fruit
5¼" dia., 5¾ oz.

Rectangular Sugar
3¼" long
2½" wide
1½" high

Covered Sugar
4 oz.
2⅝" high
3" dia.

Handled Creamer
4 oz.
1½" high
2¼" dia.

Bud Vase
5¾" high

Double Egg Cup
3⅛" high

Salt and Pepper
3¼" high
1⅝" dia.

Napkin Ring
1" wide
1¾" dia.

Souffle
6 oz.
2" high x 3½" dia.
also in 2¾", 3", and 4" dia.

Tray
6¼" x 6⅝"

Coffeepot with Lid
25 oz.
6" high x 3⅝" dia.

Soup/Chowder Mug
14 oz.

Tete de Lion Bowl
14 oz.
3½" high x 4⅝" dia.

Teapot with Lid
37 oz.
5" wide x 4" high

Ind. Teapot with Lid
17 oz.
4" wide x 3¼" high

This is the collector plate we were the first to innovate, using a metal disk on porcelain. The design was so successful it was imitated by many other decorators. The plate shown was part of the Oriental *Chokin* Series. It received the Discovery Award from the Society of Glass and Ceramic Decorators and was featured in *Gifts & Decorative Accessories* magazine, April 1984.

This plate was designed for the Youngstown Symphony for a fund-raising campaign. Artist John Buxton did the actual rendering of the design, which was based on photos of the orchestra's home, Edward W. Powers Auditorium. Each plate had an individualized message of gratitude inscribed on the back. Photo by Edward Lawrence Studio. Courtesy of *Symphony* magazine and the American Symphony Orchestra League.

Whenever we had a new pattern, new shape, or new item we got good coverage in industry magazines. If any of the items were newsworthy for the general consumer, we got good coverage in national magazines and larger newspapers such as *The New York Times* or *The Washington Post*. When we produced the china to be given to President and Mrs. Carter and to Vice President and Mrs. Quayle, our PR director sent releases, as you saw.

Targeting Public Relations

Target your PR to get the most benefit from it. Keep your PR person informed about where your customers and your reps are located so that the newspapers and magazines in those regions carry stories about your company.

Establish a reporting system and pay scale with your PR person at the beginning. The person can report to you weekly, or monthly, or quarterly. In our case, the PR person sent monthly reports and we paid a monthly fee. If she used an ad agency, we paid those additional fees.

When you attend trade shows, be sure you work closely with your PR director ahead of time to ensure that you are featured in a trade show editorial. Sometimes we had to buy ad space to get our message across, but most of the time our PR director just sent a regular press release.

Think twice before putting together media kits and handout literature for trade shows. Many companies spend thousands of dollars on media kits and promotional material to hand out at trade shows. We did it at the first show we attended. We found they were expensive and did not generate sales or leads so we quit doing it. Instead we took visitors' business cards or impressions from their trade show badges and mailed them the material they requested. By qualifying visitors while they were in the booth, we further cut down on our wastage.

Using Public Relations Creatively

Make your product available as a prop for expensive ads that other companies are buying. We did this and it paid great dividends for us. For example, if a product was being photographed for an expensive ad and the photographer needed a prop that included china, our PR director let the editors know she had china they could use. She also let them know that we would make something for them to use. We appeared in several impressive magazines that way. The magazines generally credit the products' companies. The cost was negligible and the returns in PR were great.

This pattern was featured in *Food Arts* magazine. It appeared in their Table Top section and was titled "The Snap of Black and White." I designed the Checkerboard pattern, which has been used in restaurants and bistros. Photo by Edward Lawrence Studio.

One time our PR person called and asked if we had a pattern with clusters of grapes. We told her we would create one and ship it by the end of the week. We did, and we were featured in a beautiful full color two-page spread in a design magazine. While others paid thousands of dollars for full color ads, we appeared in the same magazine for nothing. If you help the editors, they are eager to help you when the time comes.

Entering Contests

I discussed national awards as a way to promote your business. Now I want to expand on the subject to show how we did this without much cost. One of the magazines in the restaurant field gives annual awards to restaurants with the finest tabletop. Our PR director made sure we submitted photographs for those competitions. Taking photographs can be expensive and difficult. We used several techniques to solve the problem.

First, our PR director contacted the restaurateur and asked if we could have a copy of the photographs they had taken as part of their own promotion campaign. When we told them we were entering the picture in a national contest, they were eager to let us use their photographs.

Sometimes the restaurant had not planned to take pictures that would qualify for a national contest. In that case, she would convince them that if they took the pictures it would help them with their own advertising and give them a chance at national recognition if the picture won. Many times they would agree to take the photographs and pay for them.

Sometimes our PR director offered to pay half of the photographer's cost to have the pictures taken. This almost always worked. When it didn't, we paid the fee. A few times our reps also entered photographs of our china in contests.

If you enter contests, enter as many times as you can. We quickly learned the more photos you enter, the more chances you have of winning. We tried to enter in as many categories as possible because we knew that would help promote our business with customers who fit in those different categories. We won almost every year we submitted photos for the tabletop awards.

Your Product as Presentation Awards

One final way you can receive publicity from your product is to make it available for presentation awards. If it is given to important people or represents a notable event, you gain more recognition. A news release about the award generally gives information about the product. It is an excellent way to receive publicity, just for the cost of the product you give. We supplied the china for the winning design at the Carleton Varney School of Art and Design, a College in the University of Charleston. We also supplied the White House Dessert Plates that were given at fund-raising dinners for one of the political parties.

If you or anyone on your staff can write, you can get free publicity from articles you write about your company, your customers, or your product. I wrote two to four articles a year and a 500-word column for an industry magazine.

This plate was presented to President Ronald Reagan at a Republican fund-raising dinner. Photo by Edward Lawrence Studio.

You can write about anything pertaining to your company if it is relevant and can help other people in your industry. It has a better chance of getting published if you accompany your article with pictures. Some magazines use only black and white shots, but most prefer color slides.

Keep a library of color slides of your company, its products and manufacturing processes. Offer them to editors of general consumer magazines who might need them to illustrate articles. They will generally give you credit. Even if they don't, you are still ahead by being able to show the publication when promoting your company to others.

Cooperate with Editors

We were contacted by editors on two separate occasions to supply color slides for articles. One slide showed decal making; the other showed our product. If you are adept with a 35mm camera, you can take your own color slides. When we first started our business I didn't have that experience so we had professional photos taken. Later I learned with the new automatic cameras and some careful planning I could take adequate action shots of employees at work. However, I never attempted to take formal photographs of our products. That requires training and great skill to get a professional look.

Our color slide library included action shots of our process in addition to photos of patterns. Initially, we put these pictures in a small photo album we supplied to our reps. As more magazine articles were published about us, showing pictures of our company, we discarded the photo albums and relied on the company notebook that contained reprints of the articles. The pictures in those articles were actions shots I took and professional shots the photographer took.

There are many ways to utilize publicity that require little expenditure on your part, if you know how. Check out books on public relations from the library, and talk with others about how they use public relations for their business. Editors need news to stay in business. If what you are doing is news, you have something to write about. You cannot make a sales pitch in a news release or ask readers to buy. You can only talk about something new, exciting, or different. If you submit your release yourself, always send the material directly to the business editor, not the advertising department. If you are doing your own PR, it's best if you assign the PR duties to one person so that you know who is in charge and information doesn't slide through the cracks. When you contact magazines, try to work through the same one or two people at those publications.

When you do buy advertising space, show preference for those publications that have given you free publicity over the years. If you aren't buying any advertising space from anyone, let them know. You don't want them to think you are spending your advertising dollars with someone else and relying on them only for free publicity.

Trade Associations Bring Recognition

Become active in trade associations in your industry. If someone on your staff is adept at giving motivational talks, you can promote your business through association meetings. Schedule the person for a workshop or a speech. If someone on your staff is appointed chair of an association group, assemble the best speakers and do your best. Approach it as a powerful PR tool for your company.

I presented papers and gave workshops at a number of conventions and trade shows, and was keynote speaker for an international meeting. The year I was chair for the Design Division of the American Ceramic Society I made sure we honored one of the world's foremost ceramic designers, Eva Zeisel. It was another way to promote our company on an international level.

This photo was taken when I presented Eva Zeisel with the design award from the American Ceramic Society. Woodmere produced the award plate and donated it because of the publicity we knew the award presentation would receive. A number of trade publications and newspapers carried the story because Eva Zeisel is known internationally for her designs in the ceramic field.

Even if you don't become an active member of industry associations, use them to promote your business by exhibiting at their trade shows.

TRADE SHOWS

Many successful business owners believe that a good way to promote small business is through trade shows. Trade shows offer opportunities to introduce new products or patterns, meet customers, obtain reps for your company, enhance your position in the market, generate sales leads, and sometimes even sell your product.

You may want to attend trade shows and conferences as a visitor first to learn how others display their product before you compete with them. You will get the same view of the shows that the average visitor gets.

We attended a few industry shows in the commercial and collectibles field as visitors first. We wanted to learn more about those markets and see what our competition was doing. We discovered that we did not need to exhibit at collectibles shows to reach our customers. We also discovered we did have to exhibit at other industry shows to reach our commercial market.

Planning for Trade Shows

You can do several things to ensure that you have a productive trade show. First, have a definite goal. Know ahead of time what you want to accomplish and why you are going. In our case, we knew our major goal was to get good leads. In most of the markets we served, we did not make sales at trade shows.

After contacting the sponsoring organization and getting the exhibitor kit, make sure it is the type of show you want to attend. You want to know how large and what kind of audience it draws and whether it has a good reputation with your competitors. You want to know if it is a local or regional show. You may want to attend only national shows. Those were the only ones we attended unless it was for a very special regional audience.

Another important factor to consider about trade shows is where they are held, not only the city but the center itself. At one time when unions were very uncooperative in Chicago, companies dreaded to attend conventions in that city. It hurt the associations and it hurt businesses too.

Your exhibitor kit will include a floor plan and other details about the show. If it is a popular show, many of the choice booth spaces are already taken because last year's exhibitors reserve their same booths a year in advance. The first year or two we attended popular shows, we only got in when there was a cancellation. Because we were often called at the last minute, we prepared ahead as if we had been accepted. We did this partly because we believe strongly in a positive attitude and partly because we wanted the practice of planning ahead.

No matter what kind of show it is, you want to get the most results with the smallest space in the shortest amount of time. There are some ground rules you need to set for yourself and your people. First, plan several months in advance. Decide on the types of items you need to promote to reach the audience you are targeting. Your tendency will be to bring more than you need, so when you begin to plan, include everything and then begin eliminating items until you settle on those that are the most important for that particular show.

We learned you also have to bring extra pieces of what you consider the most important because something always gets broken or lost. If you have new techniques, new products or patterns for that particular market, include those and the most popular or well-known items associated with your company. Customers bring people by your booth just to show others what they bought, or what they have heard about or seen in a magazine.

If we had items that a famous person had bought, we always featured those, no matter who the audience was. It was a way to promote our image as a quality company that sold to important people. If you have been on the cover of a magazine or won an award, use it as a prop in the booth or feature it.

Practice Sessions Help

Have a practice session where you set up your booth ahead of time so you know what it will look like. You are going to the show to promote your business. You are making a sales presentation, whether you make sales there or get leads. You are presenting your company and its products to thousands of people and spending thousands of dollars to do it. Make the most of those dollars by planning your booth ahead of time. Even though you plan ahead, don't make the mistake of thinking your plan is set in stone. Be willing to vary it and improve it on the spot, at the trade show. If you see something you need to change, change it.

We were lucky that we had a large warehouse where we could set up our booth and arrange items as a dress rehearsal. We practiced arranging our booth in different ways until we had a routine firmly set for the most productive way to set up our booth, show our items, and dismantle it in an orderly fashion. We practiced assembling and dismantling our booth until we could do it in record time.

Make a diagram of your booth during the early planning stages.

Label each item and where it goes. Take pictures of your booth while you are planning it and then again after it is completed at the show. You can compare these pictures to see how you changed your display at the last minute.

Display Booths

Some companies spend small fortunes on their trade booths. We didn't and still found we could make a good impression if we were careful. We built our first trade booth for less than $2,000. Our last booth was a standard, lightweight collapsible model. It could be dismantled, packed, and ready to ship in less than thirty minutes. It was a unit that could be assembled with other units to expand from ten to twenty or more feet. The new booth cost us $2,500 for each ten-foot unit.

You can use glass, wood, or laminated tables, or expandable build-on units to display your product. Observe what your competitors and others do. You will get some good ideas you can incorporate into your booth. That's another reason to visit some shows first before exhibiting.

You may want to have special cases made for your product so that it is easier to pack and ship. It is faster if you minimize the need for packing materials. We had foam-lined Naugahyde cases made to hold the china so that it could be wrapped in protective covers, zipped shut, and put into storage barrels for shipment. The storage barrels also served as our display tables. The barrels were shipped in specially built wooden crates on wheels. Each crate was large enough to hold two barrels and miscellaneous items such as acrylic show chairs.

Be sure your company logo is large, in good taste, and expensive looking. It should be prominently displayed in your booth. We had our company logo produced in high quality brass and hung it in the center of the booth. You can rent carpet, flowers, telephone, lights, and chairs at the trade show. We rented the telephone, carpet, lights, and flowers.

Trade Show Space

You will need to contract with the convention center's labor force to help you assemble some parts of your booth. All convention centers require you to hire an electrician. Some even require you to hire a carpenter or laborer to assemble your booth, even though this may be unnecessary. We preferred to pay the laborer the fee and ask him to leave us alone. We could assemble it faster because we had developed a system. You need to check with the convention centers regarding their rules for setting up and dismantling booths.

What size booth space do you need? Booth space is normally available in ten-foot increments. At some shows, you may require twenty feet or more to show off your product. At other shows, a ten-foot space will give you as much recognition. Sometimes the space that is available dictates what size you get. At other times, cost alone dictates your booth size. Placement of your booth for traffic is as important as size. We discovered organizations usually put companies with similar products in close proximity, so shoppers can see competitive products without walking long distances.

There are advantages and disadvantages to placement. We were never placed next to a competitor, although we were often assigned space on the same aisle or three spaces from a competitor. We welcomed the competition. We thought it improved our image to compare what we did with what others in our industry did.

Try not to be directly opposite one of your competitors. This makes some prospects nervous; they may hesitate to be seen shopping your booth and your competitors' too.

One of the activities you will enjoy most at a trade show is visiting the other booths, especially your competitors'. We were eager to share ideas and to ask questions about new patterns, products, and techniques. We learned a great deal from studying the competition. We learned what to do and what not to do.

Behavior at Trade Shows

Behavior at trade shows is important if you want to promote your business and project the right image. Here are some suggestions. Arrive on time, dressed appropriately, and well groomed with a smile on your face. Have your business cards and promotional materials handy. Keep your briefcase, coats, hats, and other items out of sight. Stay in the back of the booth or on the perimeter so that visitors know you are available when they want to ask you something. Be helpful, friendly, cooperative, and genuinely interested in those who stop to talk with you. Stay in the booth for the times listed in the show catalog.

Don't eat, drink, smoke, or chew gum in the booth. Don't visit with your booth companion, your neighbor in the booth next to you, or on the telephone while visitors are in your booth. Don't leave for lunch or coffee unless you have a companion to watch the booth. If there is traffic in your booth, don't leave even if it is your turn to leave. And never leave the booth early. More than once, we got our largest order and our best leads in the last five minutes of the last day.

If you have valuables, store them in appropriate places in your booth and never leave them overnight. If you have products that you think are tempting to convention personnel, put them away overnight so they are not readily available. Come to the booth early enough each morning to arrange your product and see that everything looks good again. Your booth should look as good the last day as it does the first day.

Most convention centers have vacuuming and cleaning services provided as part of the package. Be sure this is included. We always brought a small hand vacuum to be sure our booth was clean each morning. We also brought glass cleaner and paper towels. Included in our emergency kit were hammers, nails, pliers, Scotch tape, masking tape, and a first-aid kit.

Assign someone the task of organizing the details of the show before you attend, while you are there, and when you leave. There is a great deal of paperwork involved with trade shows. If one person is in charge there are no mix-ups; if several people are responsible or if duties overlap, something will be forgotten.

Generally, you need two people to staff a ten-foot booth, three or four people for a twenty-foot booth, and five or six for a thirty-foot booth. Each person should be allowed to have a rest break every two or three hours depending on the traffic in your booth.

Your people should be trained in your product and in how to qualify leads. When a visitor comes to your booth, introduce yourself and ask where they are from. Carry on a dialogue with them. Make sure you are talking with a decision-maker, not someone who has no authority to buy your product.

After the Trade Show

Keep track of the leads you generate at shows. Don't just collect business cards and names and then forget them. Make notes regarding each lead so you don't forget details. We marked the leads with rating numbers from 1 to 3, with 1 being the best. We marked the appropriate reps' names on them and gave them to our sales service department when we returned to the office.

Call your reps and let them know you are keeping track of the leads you gave them. If we didn't check on the reps, we found sometimes they didn't follow through as rapidly as they should have. We let them know that if they did not follow through on leads, we would contact the leads and work directly with them. We rarely had to do this.

After you return from a trade show or any business trip, have a meeting to evaluate how you think you did. Although we did this informally at the end of each day over dinner, we had a formal meeting at the office later. You must keep track of all your expenses and the orders the show generates. It may be a year or more before you can actually credit shows with specific orders.

Sometimes you never can. But with some kind of record-keeping, you can get a good idea of which shows are productive and which ones are not. Just as with everything else you do to promote your business, you need to keep good records. We had all our records in the computer and set up those areas we wanted delineated. On page 122 is an example of the records we kept for trade shows.

TRADE SHOW EXPENSES AND RESULTS FOR YEAR _____

Show Locations Dates	St. Louis Apr. 9-11	Wash. DC July 15-17	Ohio Aug. 4-7	Pittsburgh Aug. 18-21
Airfare Hotel Booth Space Setup Costs				
Show Expenses Telephone Meals Entertainment Travel Miscellaneous				
TOTAL EXPENSES				
Orders Received				
TOTALS				
Total Leads Total Sales at Show Total Sales After Show Commissions Paid				
NET PROFIT				

Average Dollar
   Amount of
     Purchase Order
Average Profit
   Per Order				

NOTES:
1. Length of stay was show dates plus two travel days.
2. Show expenses were carpet cleaning, flowers, extra lights, and additional props if needed.
3. Size of booth space was indicated.

5.

Managing Trouble

Every successful business owner encounters trouble. It may be a minor disappointment, a vexing problem, or a major disaster. We endured our share of troubles when we owned our small business. When you visit with other successful business owners, you quickly learn they have too. They discuss their past troubles with a tolerance for nature's whims, or with a sense of humor at their own naivet or greed. That's because many times we invite what happens to us through lack of planning, neglect, mistakes, or bad judgment. Sometimes we are just greedy. Other times we just happen to be in the wrong place at the wrong time.

You can do everything right and still be hurt by a whim of nature or circumstances beyond your control. Sometimes those circumstances are within your control. Whether they are or not, your attitude and response determine the outcome. You won't succeed unless you can overcome trouble, whether it is a minor disappointment, a vexing problem, or a major disaster. The strategy for the small business owner is to view all troubles as hurdles to leap, not as reasons to fail.

You will find trouble doesn't occur in a vacuum. One thing leads to another, and before you know it you have not one but two or more obstacles to overpower at once. I will describe certain kinds of trouble you meet in business as disasters, others as problems, and still others as disappointments, based on dictionary definitions. A disaster is "... a sudden or great misfortune ..."; a problem is "... a source of vexation ..."; a disappointment is "... to fail to come up to the expectation of ...."

You can call them what you like. The important thing to remember is that whatever you call them, they happen to everyone in business at some time or another. After learning what we did to overcome ours, I hope you will be better equipped to deal with your problems. The purpose of this chapter is not to scare you out of business, but to encourage you to stay in business, in spite of whatever may happen to you. You won't fail if you fall down or get knocked down. You will fail only if you decide to stay down.

Dealing with trouble, whether disasters, problems, or disappointments, is a necessary part of owning a small business. How you respond determines your success. Therefore, you need to be concerned with: (1) point of view, (2) disasters, (3) problems, (4) disappointments, and (5) lessons you learn.

POINT OF VIEW

Your point of view has everything to do with how well you deal with trouble. If you view disasters, problems, and disappointments as major catastrophes that will put you out of business, they probably will. If you view them as difficulties you have to work out, you will manage. You will learn from your experiences and be strengthened by them.

What happens to you is not so important as how you react to what happens to you. Someone once said what is inside comes outside when you're squeezed. If that is so, you had better be filled with plenty of optimism, confidence, and determination, because disasters, problems and disappointments are quite a squeeze. If you aren't powered by a positive attitude, they can put you out of business.

All the enthusiasm of the salesperson, the adeptness of the marketer, and the perseverance of the entrepreneur are necessary when it comes to dealing with trouble. You need to believe in yourself, your business, and your product. Be enthused about your work. Be optimistic about the future. Be decisive about your actions. Be determined about your follow-through. It also helps to have a sense of humor.

DISASTERS

A Management Disaster

Our first disaster was our worst and came closest to putting us out of business. Yet we succeeded in spite of it. It was a personal disaster we could have avoided. It was caused by hiring the wrong person to do a job. It involved several major factors simultaneously: our building, our product, and our people.

Gene had been successfully operating our marketing and importing firm for two years when he started the decorating plant. Gene did the marketing, selling, and the financial planning. He hired a young man to run the manufacturing end of the business, which automatically included managing the people. I hired some of the employees for both companies and did some marketing and design work on a part-time basis while teaching at a nearby university.

Nine months after the plant began production, Gene informed me that it was so far behind in shipments and so poorly run, it would "go under" if something wasn't done immediately. He asked me to quit teaching at the university and apply what I had learned during my doctoral research at the large china factory. I agreed and set to work. The following description shows how bad business can get with bad management.

POOR ORGANIZATION AND LOW MORALE

The plant was a dirty, poorly run operation that was behind in shipments to all customers. It was overstaffed, undertrained, and unorganized. Basic procedures of warehousing — keeping similar units together, aisles cleared, boxes labeled and uniformly stacked—were ignored. No one knew how many items were in the plant nor where the items were, in any stage of production.

Five thousand square feet of space that had the potential of being an ideal work environment had become a clogged, dirty, dark building. Cardboard boxes, dirty dishes, leftover food, spilled coffee, and soft drink cans littered the work tables, the plant manager's desk, and the filing cabinets. Electric cords ran like spaghetti across the floors. Shelving frames that could be transformed into four-tiered units were used as one- or two-tiered units. Beautiful pieces of bone china lay strewn on ware boxes and shelves covered with dust.

China, ready for shipment, was mixed with undecorated and partially decorated china. Different patterns were mixed together helter-skelter. Different units such as cups, saucers, and salad plates were stacked unevenly together. Similar patterns for different companies, with slightly different decorations, were mixed on shelves. Dinnerware serving pieces of one pattern were mixed with place settings of a different pattern on the same shelves. Some shelves did not have labels, while others were incorrectly labeled.

Packing supplies and shipping cartons were scattered. When new supplies arrived they were set down wherever there was room. The packing station was situated in the middle of the busiest area of production. The back of the plant was filled with the debris that normally collects in a work environment — empty cardboard cartons, trash from wastebaskets, and discarded buckets and tools. The plant was also infested with mice.

The decals, our most fragile and expensive component, were

scattered throughout the plant, on a shelf under a leaking roof, and in unlabeled boxes and cases on the floor near the back door where temperature changes were the greatest (and could potentially do the most harm). Other decals were stored in the dirtiest areas of the plant, overhead near the chimneys that ran from the kilns. Everything was covered with dust.

Worker morale was low because there was no organization, no consistency in work habits, and no communication between the plant manager and his people. He was careless about keeping production records and time charts so that most workers were owed back pay.

Making Changes and Improving Morale

I hired a young woman who had trained as a medical secretary and was adept at keeping accurate records. She was enthusiastic and a hard worker. I told her the facts and promised that if we were successful and the plant did recover, she would have a good job and my gratitude. In my first book, *People, Common Sense, and the Small Business*, she recalls the experience in her letter to me in Chapter 9.

She eagerly set to work and helped me clean and organize the plant. We worked fourteen-hour days for three months to salvage what we could of the decals and the completed dinnerware. It took another six months before the crisis had passed and workers were pacified. I will briefly describe highlights to help those who may face a similar management disaster someday.

First, I talked individually with the workers to adjust their back pay. I took their word for what they said the company owed them. We also initiated accurate record-keeping for production areas to prevent future payroll problems. We knew workers were our most important commodity, and it was important to begin establishing mutual trust.

Reorganizing Production

We cross-trained workers so they could be moved between departments as needed. We combined tasks that eliminated unnecessary work and equipment. For example, we combined inspecting with plate numbering, which eliminated the need for workers to move plates on trays to another station for numbering and eliminated the need for trays. We knew people work more productively when the number of tasks they perform is reduced to a minimum.

We salvaged the decal and stored it in a room where the temperatures were more stable. We sorted the dinnerware items by pattern and added more shelves to the storage units. We arranged the warehouse shelves by company and pattern and drew a map so employees who substituted at different times could find items quickly. We knew people work more effectively in a well-organized environment.

We had additional lights installed throughout the plant, especially in production and inspection areas. We had all carts repaired, ordered extra wheels for future repairs, and had the kiln furniture irons straightened. We knew people work more consistently when equipment is maintained in peak condition.

We hired an outside daily cleaning service, initiated work habits to keep debris to a minimum, and enforced a no-food or beverage policy for work areas, and a no-smoking policy for the entire plant. It was then we established bonuses for ideas to improve us and for reporting mistakes. We knew people do their best when they are motivated and work in a clean environment.

We arranged production flow, assigning the lining area a separate room near the decal and decorating areas in the front of the plant. The kilns were farther back, so we placed the final inspection areas beyond the kilns near the packing and shipping departments, which we located in the back of the plant near the loading area. We knew work is easier when it is structured.

We inspected our work during each stage of production and eliminated the touch-up department, so workers would not rely on it to correct mistakes. We used identification marks on items during production and I.D. slips in the inspecting, packing, and shipping areas to track individual work so we could pay workers based on the quality of their work. We knew people work with more care when their efforts are recognized.

We used a color coding system for production scheduling as a visual aid to locate orders during different stages of production. When an item started through the first department it was coded blue. As it moved through the other departments it was coded green. By the time it reached the inspection area it was coded red. Later we kept track of each order on a large blackboard with colored chalk. After we gained more experience with record-keeping we used production sheets. We knew people improve most when changes occur gradually.

CHANGES BRING ADJUSTMENTS

We quickly learned which workers were most interested in their jobs and began training several as supervisors. It was fortunate we did because during the reorganization we lost the plant manager. We tried to teach him how to manage, but he was uncooperative and undermined the workers. When he quit, a few left with him and several more had to be fired later. During this period we lost seven workers, almost a third of our labor force.

By the end of the first year under our new management, the business was running smoothly. The production facility had been saved and we made a profit. We added a profit-sharing plan to our other benefits of hospitalization and major medical. The following year we added a dental program and a pension plan.

That disaster was the worst one for me. There is no dirtier work than cleaning up someone else's mess, especially a management mess, because it involves people. Managers who have to take over and clean up have a tough job. No matter how tactful or how careful you are, you cause bad feelings. People resist change and even though they know you are doing what is necessary, they rarely welcome it because it is always disruptive.

A Union Disaster

Our second biggest disaster was the next worst one for me and, once again, was caused by a bad management decision. It is a mistake many small businesses make—yielding to the temptation to expand as fast as you can. We did, and it brought a disaster small business owners fear most—and almost always bring on themselves—problems with a union.

Unions are credited with destroying small businesses. Even when they don't, they can seriously affect them. A union is a disaster you cause, in one way or another. You may have the best intentions and think you are doing everything right, but you can still be doing things that invite union organizers. Maybe you can learn from our experience.

Expanding Too Fast and a Downturn In Business

The incident happened when we expanded our labor force from around thirty-six full-time employees to over 100 with about sixty part-time workers in a few months' time. Our business was growing so rapidly we couldn't keep pace with it. We continually increased our production to meet deliveries. We were even expanding the building and had a contractor working on it.

At the same time, I was finding it increasingly difficult to hire full-time workers. Most women wanted to work part time, and our labor force was almost entirely women. In the meantime, I learned about a manufacturer nearby who had a labor force of 110 women workers, the majority of whom were part-time employees. He said it worked well for him. We were so desperate to hire people that we decided to try it.

Within a few months, our labor force had mushroomed to over 100 employees. We did not have enough supervisors and managers, and some of the ones we had were not completely trained. They were still unsure of themselves and so was I. We were working overtime every day. Soon production per person was decreasing, and our high quality was being compromised.

During this period, while we were growing faster than we had planned, we had a sudden downturn in business. I say sudden, but it really began several months before we realized it. We were producing large orders, but our profit margins were not good. Gene had taken the orders to keep the plant busy because we had such a large staff to support. To add to the problem, one of our biggest orders that had a nice profit margin didn't come through.

As our profits were declining so was our quality. The part-time workers were not effective, and it took longer to process orders. We were producing orders and losing money. We looked busy and we were—trying to stay afloat. It was crisis management.

We had several meetings with our supervisors and asked them to cut as many expenditures as possible to improve the profits. Nothing worked and by the end of the month Gene made the decision to terminate all the part-time workers. At first, the plant manager and I resisted because we had gone to the trouble of hiring them. When I finally saw the profit sheets in relation to the production and quality records, I realized two important facts. First, the more workers you have, the less production you get from each. Second, the more workers you have, the more difficult it is to maintain quality.

MAKING A TOUGH DECISION

After discovering this and what it was costing us, the plant manager and I agreed with Gene that we had to terminate all the part-time workers and a couple of the full-time workers who had become problems. We made that decision and planned to terminate them the following Monday; however, due to Gene's busy schedule we did not terminate them until Wednesday.

This is one advantage of owning a small business and having a husband and wife partnership that works. You can take drastic action immediately if you have to. We also decided to stop the building expansion. That was very costly since we had to pay for the labor and materials already used as well as some on order.

We reduced our staff of over 100 to about thirty-six. The plant manager, supervisors, and I all heaved a sigh of relief. Almost immediately production per person increased and quality improved. We produced as much with around thirty-six people as we had with over 100 and the quality was much better. The situation looked better but not for long. The local newspaper published a story about our termination and telephoned us for days seeking a comment. We refused all telephone calls from them.

THE NLRB INVESTIGATION

Within a week or two, we received a notice from the National Labor Relations Board (NLRB) informing us we were going to be investigated. The local Steel Worker's Union stated they received complaints from some workers who said we fired them because they were attempting to organize a union in our company. They never told us who the workers were. In fact, we were never permitted to face our accusers.

Of course, none of it was true, but we had to defend ourselves. We hired the best labor relations attorney in Pittsburgh, and for the next month or so we suffered through an NLRB investigation. We had to prove that we had terminated workers because of a decline in business and because the labor force was not effective. Our employees were interviewed individually, some in their homes, while we were not permitted to discuss the situation with any of them at any time. The union people could say anything about us and did. Our remaining employees received denigrating letters about our managers, and we began receiving nuisance phone calls at the office. We reported it to the telephone company and within a few days logged over thirty nuisance calls.

This disaster was doubly hard to endure because we both knew we caused it all by poor judgment leading to a poor management decision—to expand our business when we were not ready.

We were exonerated by the NLRB, and made such a good impression one representative commented privately that if all companies were as well run as ours there would be no need for unions. It was quite a commendation, considering the source, but not worth what we went through to receive it. I could not have agreed with them less. If we had been a well-run company, instead of running out of control, the NLRB would not have been there to investigate us in the first place. It was also quite a warning—don't expand too fast.

Financial Disasters and Greed

Small business owners often bring disasters on themselves through greed. To avoid getting hurt in a business transaction try to remember: if something seems too good to be true, it probably is. The problem with that advice is that sometimes a business proposition seems risky and turns out to be the smartest investment you ever made. You get a fantastic return on your money. Sometimes it occurs because of clever planning, other times by sheer luck. Since small business owners are always looking for the big deals that pay off, they often take flyers that end in crash landings. The motivation is usually greed.

We have a friend who suffered three financial disasters through a series of bad decisions involving one customer who looked too good to be true—and he was. He was a marketer of collectibles projects.

Marketers who put together collectibles projects contract with artists to supply the artwork. Then they contract with decal makers to supply the decal and with decorators to supply the decorating. All the components are combined at the decorator's plant. Even though the components may be owned by the collectibles marketer, they are warehoused with the decorator who must work with all of them.

This particular collectibles marketer was highly successful and developed many profitable projects when his timing was right. For him, decorating appeared to be a way to get rich quick. But it turned out to be a way to lose money even more quickly since he also lost much when his timing was wrong. He was noted for working fast deals that often hurt others who did business with him because they never got paid all that he owed them. He had been in bankruptcy once or twice before.

He went to our friend who owned a china decorating company in partnership. I described them briefly in Chapter 2. The partner who owned the majority of stock did not know as much about the business as the other partner, who was our friend. Consequently, the majority stockholder made the major decisions. He decided to extend a line of credit to the marketer because of the fast money he thought they could make. They decorated several projects for the marketer, and each time the marketer got a little further behind in his payments. Before long he owed that china decorating company over $100,000. When he wanted the company to decorate another project, while still owing them money, the major partner agreed, thinking it would help them collect their money. He reasoned that they could never collect if the marketer didn't continue operating his business. The marketer assured them that the newest project was a sure winner. It would have been a winner if a disaster had not sunk the project. The project involved a licensing contract with a famous movie star who suddenly died—so did the project.

Gene had warned the partners who owned the decorating company about the marketer, but they didn't listen to Gene. Instead, they extended more credit to the customer and soon found themselves with $300,000 in receivables from this one customer. Within a short time he filed for Chapter 11, and before any creditors could collect a portion of what he owed, he suffered the ultimate disaster. He died. No one got paid.

The large decal maker who supplied the decal for this man's projects also suffered great losses with him. They lost more money than the decorator despite having far more experience with his earlier bankruptcies and with large receivables. Gene was so surprised that he asked the CEO of the decal company, whom we knew well, how he could have extended so much credit, knowing the man's reputation. The CEO sighed, and with a sense of humor admitted, "Greed."

PROBLEMS

The Warehouse Fire

Sometimes major problems occur through no fault of your own. Among the many we endured, two involved our warehouses. The first was a fire in one of the warehouses we rented. We used it to store porcelain blanks (undecorated ware) and extra cartons. We were awakened one night by the fire department telling us our warehouse was burning. We arrived in time to see the building collapse. One of the volunteer firefighters, who had worked for us earlier, offered to stand guard until morning.

The next morning several of our workers and supervisors helped salvage what we could. Parents of two of the workers offered to stand guard in shifts so that looters would not take things before we could salvage what had not been destroyed by the fire.

The fire investigators never determined the exact cause of the fire. They speculated that some teenagers broke in and were smoking pot and accidentally set the place on fire. There was no evidence of arson and since we had a no-smoking policy that our employees kept, we were certain none of our people had caused it.

Proper Insurance and an Outside Adjuster Help

Our losses were minimal because china doesn't burn. The china we lost in the fire was broken by the firefighter's water hoses and the collapsing building. We cleaned the china that wasn't broken and were able to use some of it. We lost cartons and other paper products and sample cases and suffered some loss from the interruption of our business. We could have lost more.

We were lucky we had business interruption insurance. We would have suffered more without it. If you don't have business interruption insurance, I recommend you get it. It helped offset the losses we endured with that problem.

I also recommend you get an outside insurance adjuster to handle your case if you ever have a fire or other insurance claim. We hired one who was highly recommended by a friend. He agreed to work for a percentage of what he collected for us. He took complete charge of the claim, instructing our secretaries what records to compile. That left Gene free to do what he does best—market and sell for the company. It left me free to run the plant.

At first we were going to rely on our insurance agent to handle our claim. A friend advised against doing this and told us that it is to the insurance agent's advantage for that claim to be as small as possible. That's common sense. When that was pointed out to us, we called the outside insurance adjuster our other friend had recommended. We knew we had made the right decision when our insurance agent who owned the agency objected and became belligerent with me when I told him what we were doing.

We benefited in two ways. First, we felt confident, knowing the specialist was doing everything properly with only our best interests in mind. Second, the specialist knew things we didn't know about the law, about insurance companies, and about our needs. He got far more for us than we would have gotten otherwise. He earned his fee and our gratitude.

The Warehouse Wreck

The other major problem we endured involved another warehouse. One night the highway patrol called to say that a drunk driver had driven his van through the side of the building. We arrived to find the van protruding from a huge hole in the side of the warehouse. We hired a security guard to watch the building the remainder of the night until we could assess the damage.

The next morning when we examined the building, we found the majority of the damage was done to the china we stored in the areas near the wrecked van. Once again, we called the insurance adjuster and he handled the claim for us. While it took only a few days to clean out and repair the sections that had been damaged, it took more than a year before that settlement was made. We were lucky that this problem occurred in the spring when the weather presented no difficulty. It could have been worse.

Weather Problems

How you cope with major problems caused by the weather can affect both you and your customers. The following illustrates the differences between the attitude of a large business and a small business that endured the same major problem. The attitude of the large company ensured that the customers would never return. The attitude of the small business ensured that they would.

The day before a hurricane struck the Hawaiian Islands in 1980, we were staying at a small but elegant hotel on the Island of Kauai, with our daughter Linda and son-in-law Bill. Eager to get to the large hotel we had enjoyed previously on Maui, Gene and I hopped a plane and landed on Maui just before the hurricane hit, while Linda and Bill remained at the smaller hotel on Kauai.

For the next twenty-four hours we suffered in the dark with no electricity, no bath water, limited toilet facilities, no elevators, no candles, and poorly prepared cafeteria-style food. Our experience was so bad, we vowed never to stay there again. In contrast to this, at Linda's and Bill's small hotel on Kauai, the staff brought guests candles and free drinks to their rooms and invited them to a romantic dinner cooked over hibachis on an enclosed lanai. Despite the howling wind, torrential rain, and roaring waves, everyone enjoyed the evening. The guests perceived it as a romantic adventure because of the hotel's extra effort to compensate for the inconvenience of the hurricane. Linda and Bill enjoyed it so much they remained on the island during the storm and took a trek up the mountain the next day. They vowed to return to the hotel someday.

Government Problems

Sometimes you must endure a major problem with no end in sight. One family we know has a marketing company that imports most of the porcelain they sell. Recently, the owner's son told us about a problem they had when their company was investigated by customs agents. The first they learned about the problem was during a warehouse sale when customs agents arrived and began asking questions about the company's porcelain. When the owners asked why they were being questioned, the agents told them they had been reported for not complying with regulations pertaining to import duties for their products.

The owner's son said they found themselves implicated in a civil case and a criminal case against their corporation. The civil case involved money that would have to be paid to the government if it could be proved that the company had not paid the proper import duties. The criminal case involved penalties that would be levied if it could be proved that the company had acted intentionally to defraud the government by not paying import duties.

Customs agents confiscated samples of the company's ware and all records and files for five years prior to the alleged offense and began an investigation. The owners retained a criminal customs specialist as their attorney. After fourteen months, the criminal case against them was dropped, but the civil case has never been dropped. The customs agents still have all the company records. The owners' attorney said not to ask for the return of their files and records. The owner's son said they are learning to manage without them.

The owners said they learned through their attorney that their accuser was a disgruntled employee who had been terminated several months prior to the investigation. At the time of the termination, the employee threatened to close down the company to get even for being fired. The owners thought he intended to "badmouth" the company to customers and suppliers. They never imagined the former employee would be as vindictive as they believe he was.

Machinery, Equipment, and Other Problems

Machinery that your company relies on can break down at crucial moments and result in major problems. Whether a problem is major or minor depends on the size of your company in relation to the cost of the product. In the ceramic industry, kilns can break down. In the food industry, storage coolers or ovens can quit operating. In the garment industry, master cutting machines can jam.

Other problems develop because of equipment. Hot water tanks that give out during production when you need them most can be costly. If your business requires the use of hot water for production, the time you lose while waiting for tanks to be repaired can hurt your business. You have to decide whether to send part of your staff home or have them perform other tasks for the remainder of the day.

Equipment that breaks down during the busiest season is always costly. You usually have to pay extra for service companies to work at odd hours or overtime to repair the equipment. Then you pay overtime wages to your employees while they make up for the time lost during the repairs. In the meantime, your sales service staff is busy placating customers who are upset because your deliveries are late.

Sometimes components your business uses can give you problems. For example, in the ceramic industry, decal causes constant headaches for china decorators. Even using great care, some is accidentally ruined during the manufacturing process. The cost can be devastating if you have paid a company to produce 50,000 decals and don't have enough remaining to fill the order after a major problem occurs. Then you are forced to order a minimum of 1000 or more pieces of decal at far higher prices to produce the few items you need.

Other problems that plague the small business owner include: plumbing that leaks and ruins ceilings in offices below; machines that break down after warranty; electrical units that fail during peak production; service companies that don't show up when you need them most; supplies that don't arrive on time; trucks that break down during deliveries; drivers who damage your dock; vandals who damage your property; furnaces that quit in winter; fans that burn out in summer; plumbing that bursts; septic tanks that overflow; roofs that leak, etc. The list is endless. Your ability to endure these problems and the following disappointments needs to be endless too.

DISAPPOINTMENTS

Disappointments small business owners endure include unethical practices of some suppliers that you need to confront, fraudulent customers you have to pursue, deceitful competitors you must challenge, and unfair claims by workers that you have to defend.

Suppliers

Disappointments that involve unethical suppliers hurt because they involve your expectations of people you think you know. When we first started our business and our china was being produced by other suppliers, one of our suppliers wrote a letter to one of our biggest customers and tried to take the account from us by offering to supply the china directly. This occurred even though we had paid him what he asked for his work without trying to negotiate a cheaper price. Both we and our customer were disappointed in the supplier's behavior. This same supplier used the decal we were supplying him to decorate our patterns and decorated some of his own china, which he sold without telling us. When we discovered what he was doing, we decided not to use that supplier again.

We were luckier than a friend of ours who had a manufacturer's rep company. He related that when he couldn't collect $250,000 in commissions owed him, he began litigation. After several years, his attorney's fees totaled another $250,000 and he still hadn't collected the commissions he was owed. He dropped the suit and was never paid the commissions.

Customers and Competitors

We endured several disappointments with customers who didn't pay. Most of the time we were able to get the money through a collection agency. Sometimes we were left with their unshipped orders and had to warehouse the items without being able to sell them to recover our losses. The larger the unpaid debt, the more disappointing it was.

Another disappointment we endured involved a competitor who took two of our designs and used them as his own. Although we hired an attorney and began litigation, we decided it was a waste of money. We discovered someone can change one line or segment of a design and call it his own.

Workers

We had minor disappointments that involved workers with false claims. You can do everything right and still have false claims made against you. One involved worker's compensation when a woman claimed she hurt her back at work. Even though her claim was false and we had a witness to prove it, we lost the case. We also had false claims against us involving EEOC (Equal Employment Opportunity Commission) and OSHA (Occupational Safety and Health Administration).

We endured a false claim against us with EEOC when a young woman I terminated for absenteeism claimed I fired her because she was a woman and pregnant. I never knew she was pregnant. She missed work to attend hair-dressing classes after repeated warnings. Although I could show that 90% of our labor force and all but two of our managers were women, and that we had four women work through their pregnancies and return to their jobs, we still had to fight the case and pay costly attorney's fees. We won, but it cost us money and time and damaged our reputation for a while. We had to talk individually with each worker to explain the case to them so they would not misunderstand and become apprehensive.

Another disappointment from a false claim involved a worker I fired for absenteeism. She told the OSHA agent that she missed work because of the fumes in our plant. When the OSHA representative came to investigate, he recognized it as a false claim and was so impressed with our establishment he asked me to give talks for OSHA.

Some claims workers make against you may seem false to you but may be valid. Here are several examples of small business owners who suffered disappointments when claims were made against them. The results were costly for each of the owners.

A small business owner we know was misinformed about the status of artists. His accountant was not acquainted with wage and hour laws and told the owner that artists who were salaried were exempt from overtime wages. An artist who was asked to make up time after he had missed a day at work reported the company to the wage and hour office, saying that he had often worked overtime without pay and should not have to make up time missed at work. The owner learned that artists are not exempt from overtime wages and he had to pay back wages for the artist's overtime work.

Another small business owner of a garbage collecting company had to pay a large amount of overtime pay because of poor record-keeping. Some of his trash collecting routes were shorter than others, so some days the workers finished earlier than other days. He had developed the habit of reporting eight-hour days five days a week on the time cards, even though some days the employees worked longer than eight hours. He felt they averaged a forty-hour week because of the shorter work days when they collected from the shorter routes. When a worker was fired, he reported the company to the wage and hour office. The small business owner found he had violated wage and hour laws regarding record-keeping and had to pay back wages to all the employees.

LESSONS YOU LEARN

How to Avoid Trouble

Successful business owners learn from their experiences. You always learn something from disasters, problems, and disappointments. The most valuable lesson you can learn is how to avoid them. What may be classified as a minor problem by a large company is often classified as a major disaster by a small one. Therefore, you will find yourself ahead if you can avoid any trouble, especially a disaster. While you can't expect to avoid all disasters, you should strive to avoid as many of them as you can. In a previous section I gave examples of several that could have been avoided. Here are some we did avoid. They serve as valuable lessons.

We were told by our labor attorney that the NLRB told him a few of the part-time employees who were terminated actually were trying to organize a union. If the NLRB could prove that we knew about their organizing activity before we made the decision to terminate those employees, the investigation would have expanded and become more complex and costly. The outcome could have resulted in the NLRB ordering us to bring all the employees back to work with full back pay and benefits.

Take Decisive Action

We avoided that bigger disaster because we made a necessary decision to terminate all the part-time people when we did. If we hadn't, the organizers would have had time to inform us of their activities. We were wise in setting up our personnel policies so that our supervisors were actually group leaders, who worked as hourly employees and thus were not managers by the NLRB definition. So on the day of termination when a supervisor's relative who also worked for us gave her a letter from a worker declaring their intentions to organize, it meant nothing. When the supervisor handed it to the plant manager, who was a salaried manager by the NLRB definition, she was so overworked and rushed with terminating the different shifts and carrying out her other duties, she stuck the letter in her pocket and never read it until she arrived home that evening—after terminating the last shift. Therefore, no managers knew of the workers' plans to organize a union before the decision was made to terminate them. In fact, none of us saw the letter until after the terminations. If we had known and it could be proven that we knew, we would have been subject to the additional NLRB procedures described above.

Keep Accurate Records and Cooperate

Our labor attorney told us two other factors helped us avoid the bigger disaster. Our excellent business records documented our activities and validated our statements about our losses and our decision to terminate the employees. Also our availability and complete cooperation with the NLRB contributed to our credibility—we had nothing to hide.

Our ability to take decisive action during that period also helped us avoid a major financial problem. When we decided to reduce our labor force, we also decided to terminate our contract with the builder. It cost us thousands of dollars but not as much as the expansion ultimately would have cost us.

Maintain Good Relations With Workers

You can avoid some major problems by developing a good relationship with your people. When our company was still relatively new, we avoided a major problem involving decal because of one dedicated worker. She was a supervisor who called me in the middle of the night to tell me that the night manager was firing decal at an incorrect temperature. When she tried to tell the night manager, the night manager refused to listen. The supervisor was so concerned about the project, knowing we were down to our last few pieces of decal, that she called me, just to make sure of the firing temperature.

I told the supervisor she was right and the night manager was wrong. I talked with the night manager on the phone and had her change the firing temperature. The plates were fired at the correct temperature, and we completed the order with the exact number of pieces we had to deliver. We did not have a single piece of decal left. I kept the shop sample of that plate and it hangs in my home now as a constant reminder of the importance of one worker. She saved us thousands of dollars at a time when the difference between making a profit or suffering a loss was critical for our business.

Maintaining good relations with workers also helps you avoid problems and disappointments resulting from vindictive employees. Establish fair hiring policies. Be precise with your definitions of jobs, what you have available, how you will pay, and what is expected of workers. Communicate with your managers, supervisors, and employees. Implement your policies fairly and consistently, and carefully screen applicants before you hire them. Most important, document all of your disciplinary actions so that when you terminate someone he or she understands why.

Reject Greedy Schemes

You can avoid major financial problems by resisting the temptation to get rich quick. We avoided getting hurt with the collectibles marketer who owed our friend and the decal maker large sums of money. Gene knew his reputation. The man came to us first to decorate his projects and Gene wisely told him that we had to have payment in advance. That's when he went to our friend to have his projects decorated.

You can avoid some financial disappointments by being cautious about extending credit to people and by being careful not to extend too much credit to anyone. You also need to be careful taking on "easy" projects. If something looks "too easy" or "too good" to be true, it probably is.

Lessons from Disasters

When you can't avoid trouble, whether it is a disaster, a problem, or a disappointment, try to learn from it.

Learn from our disaster with the union. First, expand your business only after careful planning. Never let your labor force expand beyond what you can handle, no matter how much business you have to turn down. If you are not comfortable with your ability to control what you have and have no plans to control more, you are not ready to expand.

Second, be careful about relying on part-time workers for the bulk of your labor force. I hired workers on a part-time basis because I thought that was what they wanted. My intentions were good; the result was bad. They were not as productive because our jobs required a great deal of training. It took twice as long to train them, and it took longer for them to qualify for company benefits, such as health and dental coverage and profit sharing.

They were not on the premises long enough to become fully integrated employees. Their attitude was bad. Who can blame them?

Third, don't overwork your managers and staff for any length of time. Anyone can work overtime and do a good job for a short period, but not indefinitely. If your small business requires people to work overtime routinely, you are either unorganized or disorganized. Make some changes now—not later—or you may find yourself dealing with a disaster rather than a problem.

Lessons from Problems

You can learn from problems too. We learned an expensive lesson from a problem involving machinery we purchased. Our mistake only cost us $1,000. It could have cost us more than $10,000. It happened when we purchased a second tow motor for one of our warehouses. It was a reconditioned machine that carried a guarantee—or so we thought.

When the tow motor was delivered, the warehouse supervisor signed for it. He did not check the machine, nor did he start it. I would not have done so either because I trusted the vendor, knowing that his company used a well-known bank as the lender for financing the purchase.

The machine did not work. The vendor refused to do anything. When we had it checked by a local mechanic, we were told it was junk. I refused to pay the remainder of the bill and made them pick up the tow motor. The vendor and bank threatened to sue but never did. I still have the papers and the evidence in case they ever do.

Learn from our experience with the tow motor. Be careful what you buy, never sign a release until you are certain the item operates properly, and read the fine print on all contracts. What our supervisor signed implied that we were taking full responsibility for the machine delivered as is.

You learn to think quickly with some problems. At one of the biggest trade shows in Chicago, our vice president, who was in charge of coordinating the show, discovered she had forgotten the keys to the shipping crates. It was Sunday and no locksmith shops were open. We didn't want to break the locks so we contacted our PR director, who lives in Chicago. She knew a locksmith and hired him to meet us at the booth and open the crates. We learned always to travel with an extra set of keys and to have a better trade show checklist.

I would like to say that we did as well a year or two before when attended another trade show, but we didn't. The difference was, neither our booth nor our product arrived. We rented tables and drapes and had a sign painted with our company name. In the meantime, our office overnight shipped a few prestige pieces we displayed the next day. The first day, Gene used the catalog he always carried in his briefcase.

Naturally, we made a poor impression despite the time and money we had invested. That problem was caused by a bad shipper. We never used that company again. We learned two important lessons from that problem. Always check references for shippers who are going to be responsible for your show booth, and always check on the location of your booth a day or two before it is due to arrive.

You learn from other people's problems too. I mentioned earlier that I enjoy walking through trade shows visiting other booths, especially those of our competitors. One morning as I walked to our assigned space at a trade show, I noticed a most unusual booth nearby. Several men were feverishly gluing a place setting of china, crystal, and silver on a board and then hanging it on a wall. The three-dimensional look was startling.

I thought it was such a unique and eye-catching way to display a tabletop arrangement that I stopped and complimented them on their creativity. They both stopped working, looked at me surprised, and asked, "Do you really mean it?" When I said yes, they beamed with pride and heaved a sigh of relief. Then they told me about their trouble.

They had arrived in time to set up their booth, next to their biggest competitor. They were so sure the show would be a good one that they had over-spent and reserved a corner space. They had even arrived early to make sure everything went smoothly. To their horror, they discovered everything had arrived except the detachable shelves they needed to display their featured products.

They checked with the convention center labor force, the shippers, and their home office. A tracer was put through the shipper and the convention center but no one knew where the shelves were. They couldn't wait and they couldn't buy other units at the last minute, so they had to think creatively to display their products. They learned an innovative way to display a tabletop setting at a trade show as a result of their problem.

Lessons from Disappointments

Sometimes your luggage doesn't arrive and you have to attend a trade show or convention with what you are wearing. You learn from that kind of disappointment to travel in a business suit and a light raincoat, so no matter what happens to your luggage you can survive. The first time we attended a big trade show for our most important commercial customers, we had no luggage the first day. We considered that particular show one of the most important because the visitors were the decision makers for their companies. Our booth arrived in fine shape. The prestige pieces we were featuring looked great. We did not.

We were wearing the casual clothes we traveled in and did not have time to go shopping because we arrived just in time to set up the booth and change clothes. We looked like a company that didn't plan ahead. We learned another lesson from that disappointment. Always arrive a day early.

You can learn from every disappointment involving suppliers, customers, and competitors. You learn to be more careful dealing with them. You also learn from disappointments involving workers' claims that are made against you pertaining to government agencies, such as OSHA, EEOC, and the NLRB. Sometimes you are not at fault. Most of the time you are. Evaluate each situation when it occurs and learn from it. You will automatically cut down on the number of claims.

No matter what trouble your small business encounters, see it for what it is: something to deal with, not something to put you out of business.

6.

Surviving Success

Have you ever thought about what you would do after you achieved success? Small business owners rarely do. They are so busy striving for success that they don't think about what comes next. We never did until after we had been successful for several years. Then we began asking ourselves, "What next?"

Defining Success

After we started our business and it prospered so that we moved our offices from our home to a rented building, we never thought about whether or not we were successful. If we had, we would have said we were not—yet. Goals define where you are going, but rarely does anyone set a goal that says "success" and then clearly define it and stop striving. We certainly didn't.

When our business continued to grow and we moved to a bigger facility that we built, we still did not think about whether or not we were successful. Even when we expanded to additional warehouses and people began telling us how successful we were, we never thought about it. When we made yearly visits to factories in different countries, traveled first class on overseas flights, stayed at well-known hotels, saw exotic places, sampled fine cuisine, and met important people, we never consciously thought about how successful we were.

What is success? How do you know when you are successful? The dictionary defines success as "... a favorable termination of a venture ... the attainment of wealth, favor or eminence ..." But how much wealth is success? How much favor do you need to feel successful? How much power and prestige does it take to make you feel eminent?

Measuring Success

When Gene and I finally came to acknowledge our success as a company, we measured it in several ways. We felt successful by virtue of the image our employees and those who worked with us in our business had of us. They had a positive attitude toward us and our company. They were enthused, happy to be working with us, and dedicated to making our company the best it could be.

Suppliers who knew us and did business with us wrote letters of approval, praising us and our employees for our courteous response. Some vendors declared that our quality standards were excessively high and consequently tough to meet. None, however, ceased trying to meet our standards of excellence. Service companies in our community told others about our fine company and our employees, and said they enjoyed working with us.

Customers told others about the high quality of our products and the prompt service we gave. They complimented us and recommended us to others, which helped us build a good reputation in the marketplace. They helped us get numerous contracts through their support.

Our industry gave us many awards for our high quality, our innovative decorating techniques, and our new designs. We also received commendations from the state and the region for our economical use of utilities.

Heads of state and important dignitaries selected our china and proudly displayed it in their homes. Top restaurants and private clubs selected our product for their establishments.

Our company was growing and we were making a good profit, which we were sharing with our employees. We had good management policies; we operated with less than 2% absenteeism and less than 1% tardiness. We had the state's lowest tax assessment rate for unemployment and worker's compensation. All those things meant success to us.

You may have a different way of measuring success for your business. It may be your personal net worth, the dollar amount you sell each year, the number of employees you have on your payroll, the number or type of customers you have. It may be any number of things that make you feel successful.

Reacting to Success

You need to think about success and define what it means for your company. Be sure you define what success is for you personally too. Do not neglect measuring success for yourself. That is the real key to handling success when it comes. You have to feel you have achieved success along with your company, otherwise you will never be content, no matter what you achieve.

Many small business owners who achieve success for their company don't always survive it. Those who don't have not achieved success for themselves. They have achieved it for their company and for others. They have not accepted what they have achieved as success for themselves because they have not met a private goal.

When success comes, these small business owners tend to react in one of several ways: they over-spend, over-play, or over-work. We all have a tendency to do each of those things to some degree when we achieve success in business. But some small business owners carry those behavior patterns to excess and hurt themselves, their employees, and their businesses.

Over-Spending

We found ourselves taking employees on trips to Hawaii for meetings that could have been held as easily on the mainland. There is nothing wrong with sharing the wealth with key people who have helped you build your business. We are glad we did, but we did not overdo it as some small business owners do. We decided it was wiser to invest additional money in the profit-sharing program for everyone. That was why we avoided excessive spending.

Part of your job as an owner is to set a good example. If you become extravagant, your staff will too. If you have invested years developing frugal habits that contributed to your success, don't break those habits by squandering money after you achieve success.

Small business owners who overspend sometimes change their basic spending habits. Where they normally traveled coach for short trips and used first class, or business class, for long trips, as we did, they begin to travel first class on all trips. Then they insist that everyone who travels for them travel first class.

Private offices that were comfortably furnished now become sumptuous. Small "get-togethers" escalate into lavish parties. Eventually, profits begin to decline and workers resent the conspicuous expenditures, unless salaries rise commensurate with management's spending sprees. What was a small, economically-run business is now a spendthrift organization.

One direct sales company we worked for kept remodeling their company's headquarters until they had spent millions creating a miniature theme park on company property. They took employees on fabulous trips and spent money extravagantly at conferences and business meetings. Top executives had their choices of private spas, specially built electronic entertainment centers, or miniature gyms as perks. Profits that might have been shared with everyone were spent on managers at the top of the organization. Is it any wonder what had grown from a small business to a multimillion dollar corporation eventually declined and went out of business?

Over-Playing

Other business owners who have trouble surviving success take it easy. After they achieve success, they rest on their laurels. They sit back and quit doing the things that made them successful. Where they normally came to the office each day on time, they begin coming in late several mornings a week so they can play a quick round of golf. Then they begin taking days off during the week so they can play more golf or tennis. They no longer take a personal interest in the day-to-day operation of the business. Policies they implemented consistently and fairly are now sporadically applied or not applied at all. They delegate their duties but not with any planning. They just let others take over so they aren't bothered. What was a small well-run organization is now a poorly managed company.

We know one small business owner who had a business similar to ours. As he achieved success, he quit working regular business hours. He hired someone to act as his administrative assistant so he wouldn't have to be bothered with daily decision making. When he had a sharp downturn in business, he did not personally take charge, but left it to his assistant to solve the problem. When his company began to have personnel problems, he ignored them until they became serious. By the time he got involved, his employees had voted in a union, which he felt hurt his business.

Over-Working

Other business owners who have problems with success work at a steady pace until they achieve success, at which time they begin overworking both themselves and others. Instead of quitting at a normal time, they work overtime every night and on weekends, expecting others to do the same. Key people begin staying a little longer each day until everyone feels compelled to work long hours like the boss in order to keep pace with him.

Before long, no one is having as much fun working for the company, even though they are making overtime wages. What had been a company with enthusiastic workers and high morale becomes a hard-driving business with overworked employees and crisis management. When work ceases to be fun, it becomes work.

We almost fell into that trap when we expanded too fast. We had a natural tendency to overwork during our tenure as owners of a small business. Gene enjoys work, as do I. When you enjoy what you are doing, you run the risk of becoming obsessed with your work to the exclusion of everything else. Guard against that tendency, and you will have more fun as you achieve success.

Business owners who fall into the traps just described do so because they don't plan ahead for success. The problem is, success is relative. We measure success by how the outside world values us, but more important, by how we value ourselves. I mentioned executives of Fortune 500 companies who are not successful and small business owners who are. The reason is attitude.

Define Your Own Success

If you think you are successful, you are—no matter what you have achieved. People who feel they are failures measure themselves not by what they have achieved but by what they have *not* achieved that they had hoped or wanted to achieve for themselves. Therefore, if you think you are not successful, you aren't—no matter what you have achieved for your business or for others.

Each of us can be successful every day we live. We set goals; some we reach and some we don't. Striving for one thing may mean success, while achieving another thing may not. We are successful only if we think we are. Being successful is being able to recognize, acknowledge, and accept what represents success for us as individuals.

Try to keep pace with your success. Know what success is for you personally and accept it. Then recognize and accept what success is for your company. They may be two completely different things. In many cases they are.

Factors to consider when surviving success are: (1) whether to expand or maintain, (2) when to sell your business, (3) how to sell your business, (4) transitions to make, and (5) whether to consult.

EXPAND OR MAINTAIN

Small business owners rarely set dollar goals as markers for success with the notion of stopping when they reach them. They continue to set higher and higher goals. The purpose of goal setting is to achieve more in order to succeed. If that is the case, where do you stop?

Entrepreneurs are goal oriented by nature. By the time they have spent years in corporations where goal-directed behavior is rewarded and marketing strategies are aimed at achieving more,

more, and still more, they are programmed to expand what they have—not to maintain it.

What Is Too Big?

When you are successful, you have to know how big you want to grow. You may have a business that is limited either by the government or by some other force beyond your control. Unless other factors control how much you can grow, you need to decide for yourself just how big you want to be. How large is too large?

There are hundreds of success stories about small businesses that have become big businesses. In fact, the largest corporations employing thousands of people were once small businesses. The Small Business Administration in Washington, DC lists small businesses two ways: by gross yearly income and by total number of employees. This varies by industry. A retail business may net as much as $13 million a year and still be considered small. Another rough rule of thumb measures a small business as one employing 500 workers or fewer. That is a big opportunity for you to expand and still be considered "small."

You have to decide what is "big" for you. You also have to decide what is too big for you. I described some of the problems that can occur when you expand too fast without planning. I related one of our disasters when an NLRB investigation occurred because we expanded too fast.

You need not have the problems we had if you plan ahead, and I mean way ahead, at the time you start your business. We didn't plan. Gene's notion of how large he wanted our business to become was different from mine. In addition, he didn't have a clear notion of how large he wanted the company to become before selling it.

Maintaining the Status Quo Is Difficult

It is difficult to maintain a constant dollar amount of business for any length of time. You cannot predict what will happen to any market. Big accounts you thought would come through don't materialize. Other accounts that were nebulous in the planning stages come through in larger amounts than you anticipated. Your business always runs in peaks and valleys to some degree.

I planned our manufacturing operation so that we did not have layoffs after the first year or two in business. We organized our work efficiently and cross-trained employees so that when one department was slow the workers moved to another. We saved low priority jobs for those times when business was slow. We saved some jobs that we might have given to outside contractors for ourselves to do during slow periods. We solved the problem of keeping fifty employees busy all the time.

The major job of a good business owner is to gauge the market so there are as few ups and downs in the business as possible. You must constantly plan so that your overhead is covered and your inventory and receivables are not too large. At the same time, you must market your business to meet the challenges in your industry, or you will lose your niche in the marketplace.

As you grow, you need to purchase additional equipment even though your other equipment may not be paid for yet. The more you grow, the more you buy to keep pace with that growth. Before you know it, you have pyramided your debt beyond what is comfortable for you.

You need to have a comfortable margin to cover the unexpected emergencies and disasters that happen to every business. Your goal is to provide enough business so that all of your employees work with a comfort level that assures them they will continue to have full-time employment.

The market dictates to a large extent what you do and how well you do. For example, I discussed earlier the times when our customer base shifted and we had to adopt new goals and adapt old ones to meet that challenge. At one time we changed our goals so that we could operate our business with fewer people. We did this after our unplanned expansion led to severe problems for our business.

When we let ourselves expand out of control, I was fearful of growing, and I knew we did not have enough trained personnel to manage a labor force that had doubled in a few months. Yet I went along with the rapid expansion.

During that same period, Gene was so busy with the new customers he was developing, he was not able to watch the accounting end of the business as closely as he generally did. We had hired a new in-house accountant who was still learning about our business, so he and Gene were not communicating as effectively as they did later.

Plan Before Expanding

Learn from our mistake. If you are going to expand your business, plan ahead. If you have partners, all of you must understand what expansion means and how rapidly you are going to do it. You all have to agree. Then you need to prepare your management staff for what is going to happen.

You need to prepare your employees too. They need to share in any new plans. Your employees came to work for a small company. You told them you would grow and prosper. You did not say how much or how fast. The more carefully you prepare for expansion, the more successful it will be. This is especially important if your business is a partnership. Partnerships are great when they work. Husband and wife partnerships are the best of all when they work like ours did. But with any partnership there are differences. Good partnerships work because the partners complement each other. To complement means to bring something different to the relationship. Those differences are what make each partner valuable. They are also what lead to disagreements.

I mentioned that we consciously decided to change our customer base at one time after the union problem. We knew it required a certain dollar amount for us to make a profit. We also knew that the more expensive the items we sold, the fewer items we would have to produce. The fewer items we had to produce, the fewer people it would require to produce them. I discussed this in detail under "Your Quality Standard" in Chapter 3.

We decided to shift our customer base to an even higher priced, higher quality market rather than rely mostly on the less expensive, less profitable collectibles field. This was a wise decision and one with which we were both satisfied. We coasted with that business for several years. I say "coasted" because we did not work to expand our business. We worked only to maintain it.

During that period, Gene was constantly frustrated because he had opportunities to get large orders in the collectibles field, but he turned them down because our production schedules did not allow for large contract decorating if we were going to meet the schedules of our more lucrative accounts.

The majority of our disagreements during the fourteen years we were in business together centered on our differences about whether to expand or maintain the business. Gene always wanted to expand, and I always wanted to maintain what we had. I won him over for only that short period after our initial expansion got out of hand.

WHEN TO SELL YOUR BUSINESS

It's time to sell your business when you no longer want to be active in the business, even from an ancillary position. Different factors lead small business owners to make the decision to sell. You may want to sell your business when you have achieved the success you wanted or when you want to achieve something else. You may want to retire and vacation for a period of time. Or you may want to start another business. You may want to join a large company and become an employee again. Whatever your reasons to sell, you should never sell when your business is down. Hopefully, you won't have to.

Alternatives

Some small business owners don't sell their businesses. They hire others to run them while they maintain some control over the business. Neither of us ever considered hiring others to run our total operation while we owned it. We knew that when Gene no longer wanted to run the marketing and financial end of our business on a full-time basis, we would sell the business.

Before we decided to sell our business, I had developed my replacement but Gene had not developed his. He felt the marketing and entrepreneurial end of the business was too tenuous for us to hire someone else to do it. Neither of us could picture him sitting on the sidelines checking every design, second guessing every idea, and worrying about the cash flow. Gene wanted to run the marketing and financial end of our business full time or not at all.

There are other alternatives to small business owners whose business grows beyond what they want to manage. Aside from hiring someone to run it, you can turn it over to your relatives. You may find that your relatives want to work in your business and will run it the way you have. If you plan to transfer your business to someone else in the event of death, retirement, or incapacity, you need a succession plan. Small business owners rarely do any succession planning, but they should. When you do yours, get both your CPA and your attorney to help you with your plan. They can guide you in estate planning, the sale of your business to outsiders or to family members, or a liquidation of the business, and will recommend contingency provisos to cover the worst-case scenario, in case you are incapacitated. We had our advisors help us with those things.

Deciding to Sell

When we discovered our daughter was not interested in running our business, we decided to sell it. The decision to sell came about because I was becoming increasingly aware of my need to write. I decided I would leave the business. I had developed my replacement two different times. Earlier, I had developed a vice president who left after she got married. Then I developed another vice president who remained and could take over for me. I knew I could work part time or not at all in the business, even if Gene needed to work full time or not at all.

When I told Gene that I had definitely decided to leave the business, he decided to retire. He wanted to have more time to pursue his hobbies, especially fly fishing. He pointed out, however, that doing so would require selling the business. He also pointed out that if we wanted to sell the business, we would have to put it in a growth mode first. He said we would never receive the full value of our business unless it were growing.

We had purposely held our business at a certain size to support a small labor force while making a good profit. We knew that but, as Gene wisely pointed out, investors would not believe that story. We had to show them we had a viable business that could grow and grow while continuing to make a good profit. We had to prove that by expanding our business.

I asked how long it would take to expand the business. He thought that if we showed a growth period for three years, we could sell the business for what he thought it was worth. I agreed to expand the manufacturing operation and the labor force, and we put our business into a growth mode.

Planning Ahead to Sell

This time we expanded based on careful planning. I was not fearful because I knew we had an adequate management team. I also knew we would not double our labor force in a few months. We would do it over a period of a year or more. During the next three years, our business grew more than 25% a year and our labor force expanded from thirty-six to sixty. We continued to make good profits and were becoming even better known in our industry and the market.

If you decide to sell your business, take a good look at it first, not from your perspective but from the perspective of a potential buyer. If you have been coasting along, showing no growth for several years, you will need to expand your business. When you do, be sure you have a plan. Know why you are doing it. Maybe you want to expand it to get more investors. Maybe you want to expand it so that you can franchise what you do. If you decide to expand, be careful that the expansion will bring you the success you want.

If you decide to maintain your business, be aware that if and when you do decide to sell, you will need a plausible explanation for why the business has remained relatively stable without growth. You need to be able to show good profits while the business remained stable without growth.

You may want to do what we did and consciously put your business into a growth mode before putting it on the market to sell. Whatever you decide, do so consciously. Don't let yourself drift without conscious planning or you may find your success slipping from you.

HOW TO SELL YOUR BUSINESS

Evaluate Your Business

If you have decided to sell your business, you need to be sure you have something someone wants to buy. There are software programs that can evaluate your business and recommend a selling price based on a number of different factors. Your accountant may also be able to help you with this. In our case, we did not find such programs useful because of the complicated nature of our design work.

Every small business owner thinks his or her business is the greatest business in the world or, if he is bored with it, he may think it's the worst business in the world. The truth is somewhere in between these extremes. Your job is to package your business as attractively as possible and sell others on what it can do for them. You marketed your business to make it successful. Now you must market your business to sell it.

Remember Gene's approach at the bank and how he constantly promoted our business with them. You need to do the same thing with investors and potential buyers. You need to be careful, just as you were at the bank, and not oversell them on your personal contributions. They must feel they can do the job as well as you can. Many potential buyers believe they can do it better, or they would not want to buy it. They must feel they can run it at least as well as you do, or they won't be interested.

You need to make a sale—the biggest sale of your life. If you have been promoting your business effectively, you have all the tools to impress prospective buyers. You have your catalogs, employee manuals, press releases, customer base, reliable suppliers, good reps, enthusiastic employees, and good financial statements. You have all the raw materials necessary to impress a prospective buyer. Your financial statement, by the way, should be recast to reflect the profitability of the business as if it had been run by another owner with hired management. Your accountant can show you how to do this.

Look for the Right Buyer

Many people are eager to buy small businesses. There are investors everywhere looking for small businesses that are well run, have good employees, have a good track record in their industry, and can grow. If your company has a good reputation in your community, your industry, and your market, you can sell it at its true value.

If you have been promoting your business diligently, you probably have a wide network of contacts to put the word out that you are ready to sell. In fact, if you have been doing a good job of marketing your business and promoting it, you may have been approached by people who want to buy your business just as we were.

Once we achieved a certain amount of success and prestige in the industry, we were repeatedly approached by others who wanted us to sell our company to them. Some wanted us to sell it to them and remain as employees to run it. Gene and I never even considered that option. We were having fun running the business together. Why take someone on board only to work for them? You may want to, but it is hard to imagine why, unless you are short of cash. Others wanted to buy our business and run it themselves, but they didn't want to pay us what we thought it was worth.

What your business is worth is relative. Several ratios are used. Some say your business is worth five or even ten times its annual earnings. Others base the value of the business on its asset value or the years it has shown profits.

Business Brokers

When we got serious about selling our business, we discussed it with our corporate attorney who sent us to a major bank in Pittsburgh. We contacted their acquisitions department and had the bank make an assessment of our business. In retrospect, this was a waste of money. The bank never made a contact for us, and the assessment was quite expensive.

We did something else that was costly but gave Gene information he believes was valuable. We contacted a company specializing in selling businesses. There are many such companies. They usually want a non-refundable fee to search for a buying company. Gene contacted such a company through a classified ad in *The Wall Street Journal* and attended the company's business sales seminar. Later he paid the selling company's consultant to try and sell our business for us. The cost was substantial, and we got nothing from it. I would not recommend going this route. However, what Gene learned at the initial seminar did help sell the business.

For example, in the seminar they suggested what to do and what not to do. They warned against emphasizing what Gene as the owner had done to build the business. They reminded him that if the prospective buyer gets the idea that everything hinges on one person, the buyer is less likely to want the business than if he believes the company can run without the former owner.

They said the business becomes more salable if, when a prospective buyer asks how something is done, the owner says,

"Jane does that all the time. Let me have her answer your question." Even when the owner knows the answers, the more he defers to his people to answer questions, the more he conveys the idea that the company can run without him.

They also told Gene that a new owner wants to buy a business for its future growth, not its past history. Yesterday's sales and profits are just that—yesterday's. A new owner cannot rely on them for his future earnings. Recent growth, however, does show that the business is solid and thriving and has potential for the future.

Recast Your Financial Statements

In planning to sell a business, it is helpful if the owner recasts his last three to five years' annual profit and loss statements, taking out all the perks he, as owner, received from the business. You may, as we did, have an employment agreement that pays you commissions and/or bonuses beyond the amount a hired manager of the business would receive. Recast this as if the new owner hired a new manager to run the business. Possibly your car and its operating expense are charged through the company, and they might not be if a new owner hired a manager to run the business.

If you have a profit-sharing plan, as we had, you might pull that amount out as it is a discretionary expenditure. Also, your business interest expense might be recast and taken out, as that is also a discretionary expense for the new owner. Your accountant can help you do this. You may be surprised at the difference all this makes in the profitability picture your company now conveys. This is the way a prospective buyer needs to view the business.

In addition, you should put together a five-year financial forecast, assuming a new management that has no cash flow constraints as a footnote to this assumption. You must assume the new owner has no such constraints. Combine this five-year financial forecast with a dialogue detailing the plan for achieving these results. You want the forecast to be a positive one, but realistic and achievable with good management.

These recast financial statements and your five-year forecast, along with a history of the business, comprise your Offering Document for your company. With this in hand, you should begin examining the market for selling your business. Begin asking yourself, "Who is a prospect?" One of your competitors? One of your suppliers? An overseas buyer? Begin making a list of all the potential prospects you can think of and continue to add to it as you can. Below is a sample of our Offering Document.

OFFERING DOCUMENT

History of the Company: 5-10 years
    Narrative Description
    P&L's (Recast) and Balance Sheets
    Explanation of Recast Items
    Special Highlights
        A) Low Bad Debt Ratio
        B) Earnings
        C) R&D for Special Projects or Techniques

Market as It Exists Today
    Sales by Type
    Sales by Region
    Sales by Each Competitor

Market as You Forecast It 5 Years in the Future
    Sales by Type
    Sales by Region
    Sales by Each Competitor

Plan for Future
    Narrative Description
    Sales & Earnings Forecast

Summary of Strengths
    Location
    Physical Facilities
    Equipment & Computerization
    People
    Patents & Copyrights

Unique Advantages

In our case, we began contacting everyone we knew and ultimately found someone who was in touch with large corporations that were looking for companies like ours. The contact told one of the corporations about us and they sent someone to check us out.

Tours Help Sell Your Business

You can also enhance the process of selling your company by implementing a visitor's policy that includes guided tours. If you don't have a such a policy, establish one. I mentioned this briefly when discussing promoting your business, but it is important to emphasize it again. Guided tours help promote your business when you are building it and help market it when you are selling it.

Well-conducted guided tours impress everyone who visits your company. They show you are a well-run organization and impress prospective buyers. Remember, anyone can be a prospective buyer or can know someone else who may be a prospective buyer. People who visit your company tell others about it, which can result in the sale of the product or the sale of the business itself.

We had a visitor's policy in which everyone registered when they arrived. Then they were given a tour emphasizing areas of particular interest to them. The tours were given by different people and were basically the same with only slight variations that emphasized those aspects of special interest to that particular visitor. We found this a good way to promote our business when we were building it and also when we were selling it.

When prospective buyers began visiting our company, Gene insisted on personally taking them through the entire facility. He knew that he was trying to make a sale and he wanted complete control over the sales presentation. His rationale was sound. You generally don't make a sale with different salespeople handling the presentation of your product. On the other hand, following the advice of the expensive consultant, it might have been wise to let me take prospective buyers through the manufacturing facility, let my replacement take them through the office, and let the accountant take them through that department. You need to make such decisions ahead of time.

We had a series of visitors who were prospective buyers. We had opportunities to sell our business several times; however, some of the prospects didn't have the cash to support the business, and others didn't have the knowledge or experience to continue running our business effectively.

Check Buyers Carefully

You may think we were too particular when deciding to whom we would sell. We wanted to be sure our employees would be taken care of when we left. We felt a responsibility to them as well as to the customers we had serviced. We had a reputation in the industry and in the marketplace. We also felt a sense of pride in what we had created, and we did not want to see it mismanaged or destroyed. We were not trying to make a fast dollar. We were trying to provide for the future of our company and our people. We wanted to be sure the buyers were worthy of what we had to sell.

Here is an example of what can happen when you don't take special care when you sell your business. One small business owner we know had a successful wallpaper and fabric store. After her husband became seriously ill, she decided to sell the business so she could spend more time with him. One of her employees recommended someone she knew who was interested in buying a small business.

Since the prospective buyer was recommended by an employee, the owner did not conduct a thorough investigation. She did not pursue references beyond talking with the man's banker and getting a financial statement. She did not check with other people in the community to learn more about the prospective buyer.

When she told the buyer what she wanted for the business, he did not attempt to negotiate a cheaper price. He did say, however, that he preferred to make a small down payment and work out a monthly payment schedule for the remainder of the price rather than invest a large amount initially. She agreed.

Within a short time, he refused to make payments, stating that the debts she listed on the purchase agreement were less than the actual debts. He also said that the receivables were not adequately covering the company's debts. She hired an attorney and began litigation.

In the meantime, she learned that the buyer had a reputation for nefarious dealings in the community. She took him to court several times but he never appeared. Her case has been pending for over a year. In the meantime, the buyer is operating her business as owner and making a good living. The previous owner is still waiting to be paid.

Other Complications When You Sell

You can investigate the prospective buyer and still have problems selling your business. We know someone who had a business similar to ours. His manufacturing operation included land that adjoined his factory. He was told he had to have Environmental Protection Agency (EPA) approval of the land to ensure there was no toxic waste involved. The final closing hinged on federal clearance.

For two years he could not get EPA approval because the EPA would not set up the guidelines for that approval. When they finally did state what had to be cleared by inspection, the seller and the buyer each agreed to pay half of the cost to have the land inspected. However, the buyer did not pay his share.

In the meantime, the seller has been unable to complete the final closing and is still running his business. He doesn't want to turn it over to the buyer because the buyer has not paid his share of the cost of having the land inspected. The buyer, on the other hand, is also reluctant to close the deal. This predicament has dragged on for six years.

Those kinds of experiences can happen to you if you are not careful when you begin marketing your business to prospective buyers. As the owner of a small business, you have an obligation to find the best prospect you can. If you have built a good business, you have the respect of your people, your customers, and your industry. You now have a responsibility to see that your business continues to operate with the same basic values you established.

You cannot guarantee that new owners will run the business exactly as you did. Everyone brings his or her own management style to the job. You can try to ensure that the buyer is honest, has integrity, and will respect what you have built. Do that, and you will have achieved your final goal—providing for your succession.

TRANSITIONS

When you sell your business or leave it to retire, you and your employees will undergo a transition period in which all concerned will experience some emotional stress. Your transition from owner to non-owner can be bumpy if you are not prepared for it. Your employees can suffer feelings of insecurity too. The more closely you have worked with your employees and shared decisions with them, the easier the transition will be because you have developed mutual trust. They know you will not misrepresent what will transpire.

Plans for the Transition

Feelings account for part of the adjustments you have to make. Habits of behavior account for another part. Working together every day, you establish habits that are hard to break. You will miss the day-to-day decisions you made with others, the excitement of a new account, even the pressures of developing a new program for your operation.

Business is always in a state of flux. You never leave a business with every task completed. There are always projects that need to be developed, problems that need to be resolved, opportunities that need to be investigated, people who need to be placated, customers who need to be cultivated, and employees who need to be counseled.

Before you leave, you should prepare yourself and your employees for the transition. They have worked for you for years—now you are leaving. They wonder what the new owner will be like. They wonder if the new owner will be as patient as you are. They know how you react in most situations. Over the years you have built a spirit of comradeship and loyalty, and all of you will miss that. But you have an advantage over your employees. You are leaving. You do not have to adapt to a new owner and another manager. They do. No one likes change. It is disruptive and uncomfortable, especially when it is beyond your control.

The more carefully you plan the transition with your people, the better. If you have investigated the new owners before selling to them, you know their good points as well as their weaknesses. You need to promote the new owners' image with your people as soon, and as often, as possible.

The good job you did promoting your company's products with customers accounts for its success. The good job you did promoting your business with prospective buyers accounts for its sale. Now you have to continue your good job of promoting to ensure a smooth succession. You want everyone to be satisfied and comfortable with the new relationship.

You have sold the buyer on your company and your people. Now you have another selling job. You have to sell your company and your people on the buyer. You spent years developing a good, cohesive labor force. That is part of what the new owners bought. Make sure you don't leave them with a confused, resentful group of people instead of the enthusiastic team you introduced them to when they first visited your facility. You owe it to your employees and to the new owners to make the transition as smooth as possible.

When to Tell Your Employees

When do you tell your people that you are selling? We told our top managers and supervisors as soon as we made the decision to sell. That was several years before the actual transaction. Our management style was based on mutual sharing. We wanted them to know why we were selling and how long it would take.

Telling them about our decision to sell justified our decision to expand the business. We had spent several years showing them that smaller is better. Now we were going to ask them to expand because bigger was going to be better. They had to know why. We told them we wanted prospective buyers to be aware of our company's potential for growth and our employees' potential for growth.

Our employees knew we had numerous opportunities to sell in the past but had not done so. We told them we were waiting for the right buyer so that they would be taken care of. While we could not guarantee the business would be exactly the same, we wanted them to know we were doing everything we could to keep the company as nearly the same as possible.

When you decide to leave your business, confide in your people. If your management style has included mutual sharing, they will expect you to confide in them. Be as honest and open as you can. You will find they will support what you want to do. They may be doing so out of necessity, but if you have a good relationship with your people, they will stay with your company after you sell it. They will trust your judgment in selecting the right buyer. They will wait to see what the new management is like before deciding to leave. The rest is up to the new owners and managers.

Employee Concerns

Our employees made the initial transition with little difficulty. They had only one concern. Would the new owners be gender biased as in some companies they knew about? Their apprehension was brought about by the nature of our labor force— 90% women—and because they had experienced gender bias in jobs before. Even working at our company, they endured some gender bias from service companies. We frequently found ourselves complaining to service company owners, because the men who came to make repairs refused to discuss service problems with our staff—they were women. They would bother Gene with questions about the plumbing or electricity.

Gene finally called the owner of one of our service companies and explained that if the service reps didn't start dealing with our managers, who were women, and stop bothering him with problems he knew nothing about, we would take our business elsewhere. Even our first vice president had to contact the regional office of a major delivery service to complain about the discrimination our shipping clerk endured from their male driver.

With that as background, it was natural that our people were uneasy at first. Our employees' fears proved groundless, because the new buyers were good people with integrity. Nevertheless, new owners represented a big change for them and it was good that we had agreed to stay a year after the sale to help everyone make the transition. If you prepare ahead, you will have as smooth a transition as we had.

WHETHER TO CONSULT

After you sell your business, you may find you have an opportunity to continue lending your expertise to your industry or your company by consulting. Two factors determine whether or not to consult: your need and the company's. You may want to consult because you find it difficult to adjust to a different lifestyle after selling the business, or because you need additional income while you adjust. If your business is highly technical or creative and the new owners are not experienced in your field, they may want you to consult for a short period.

Consulting Benefits Everyone

Consulting gives the new owner an opportunity to utilize the talents of an expert while giving the expert an opportunity to help the new owners. Each of you has a vested interest in the company's success. Unless the new owners paid you cash or a very large down payment with a short payment schedule, you will have to wait a year or more for your total payment.

Even if the new owners have paid you cash, you still have a vested interest in your former company. After all, you created the business and made it successful. Your company produced a good product and provided steady jobs for a number of people. It's only natural for you to want your company to continue being successful.

Another factor that affects whether or not you consult is how long a transition period you and the new owner have after you sell the company. Most new owners prefer to take over completely from the beginning. Maybe that's because there is some truth to the saying that former owners make the worst employees. In those cases, the former owners have little or no contact with their companies after they sell. Others who sell are put on a retainer, or consult for a short period.

We agreed to run the company for one year after the sale while the owners searched for Gene's replacement. We also signed a five-year non-compete contract, which included consulting. Consulting can take several forms. You can work full time sporadically, part time consistently, or work only when called. We agreed to a maximum of 300 hours a year if they needed us.

Gene had spent thirty years as a marketer in the industry and was highly respected. He had a wide network of business acquaintances who were valuable to the company. The longer the new owners and the company could draw on Gene's knowledge and contacts, the better off they would be. We recognized that and agreed to consult. I had little to do except for some designing, since the replacement I had developed for manufacturing was doing a good job.

Helping Out When Needed

One of the duties we initially had before moving to Florida was helping the new owners find Gene's replacement. That was a big undertaking. We recommended several people to them. Our first choice was not theirs. The man they hired did not work out and within a year and a half we were using all our consulting hours to help them find another replacement. In addition, Gene did almost all of the marketing for them. He was able to do most of it by telephone. However, we both attended trade shows and visited clients and vendors to reestablish the company's networks.

We spent some time at the company and visited with the employees to get a first-hand picture of what the company looked like after our year and a half absence. The marketing end of the business had suffered, and the employees were apprehensive about what had transpired. The labor force had shrunk, but the management policies were still in place and the factory was still producing a good product. The replacement I had developed for my end of the business had endured the past year and a half with grace and fortitude. Within a short time, everyone was comfortable again. Six months later, the new owners had hired another replacement for Gene's end of the business and also an excellent marketing consultant. The new manager was compatible with the employees, and the company was once again running smoothly.

Reestablishing the networks with foreign suppliers was more time consuming. We had developed a very close relationship with our Japanese suppliers. Fourteen years is a long time to work together. When you are located on the other side of the world, it is not easy to make visits, so you communicate by fax and telephone. When something goes wrong, it is more difficult to adjust. It took many phone calls, a visit with the Japanese at a trade show in New York, a visit from them to our former company in Pennsylvania, and a visit by us and the new manager to their factories in Japan before they were comfortable again. While we were in the Orient, we also showed the new manager how to find new suppliers in different countries.

Consulting Helps You Adjust

Our agreement to consult helped our former company and the new owners overcome some initial difficulties. It also helped Gene make the adjustment from entrepreneur to private citizen. My adjustment occurred during the transition before we moved. Once we got to Florida, I was so busy writing my books and magazine column I didn't feel restless.

Gene did feel restless at first, despite the good fishing. His interest in the business and his daily habits, such as checking *The Wall Street Journal* for the dollar/yen relationship and talking on the telephone frequently to clients and business friends, were hard to break. He was so imbued with the work ethic and so accustomed to working in the china business that he could not stay idle.

While he was consulting for the company, he decided to explore a small niche in the porcelain market to help the company sell extra inventory. He developed that small niche market into a good, profitable business for the company during the first year and a half we were retired. It gave him an opportunity to wind down from working long hours in our business, and it gave the company an opportunity to open a new market.

We are glad we agreed to consult. When you leave your business, you may want to have a contract to consult for the new owners just to further ensure their success. Consulting may also help ensure your success as a retired business owner, making your transition from entrepreneur to private citizen easier.

Preparing for Retirement

Large corporations often prepare their workers for retirement with workshops or counseling. The small business owner has no such preparation. Right now you may be so overworked and stressed you cannot imagine being bored or at loose ends. What you may not realize is that the work habits you have spent years developing don't leave you. You need to plan how you are going to channel those habits into constructive areas that will give you some personal satisfaction. Otherwise, you will find yourself not enjoying what you strived to attain.

Some small business owners are never able to let go completely. We know several retired businessmen, physicians, and attorneys who got bored after a year or two and either got jobs closely related to what they had done before or went back into business on a part-time basis. You may want to do that. Or you may want to do what we did and channel your energies in different directions.

Gene could go on forever finding niche markets and developing them for the company, but there comes a time when you need to phase out by changing directions. Before we retired, Gene spoke wistfully of his desire to fish every day. He is an avid fly fisherman, takes fly-casting lessons, ties flies, and enjoys collecting books for his extensive fly-fishing library. He enjoys his hobbies and pursues them as eagerly as he does anything that interests him, but I knew it would not be enough. He needed something more challenging for the future years.

I asked him to act as my financial advisor and handle my investments. Even though he knew very little about the stock market at the time, I trusted his business judgment and his ability to learn quickly. I knew he would study diligently to acquire the additional skills he needed to handle my portfolio. I also knew he would have a vested interest in the project and channel his energies in that direction, which would benefit both of us.

We enjoy the new directions we have chosen, but we are still available to our company if they want us to consult. Consulting helped us make a smooth transition. They are operating efficiently now and don't call on us except to visit. We will always have an interest in our company and its people. We still turn over plates in restaurants to see who produced them. I think we always will.

We were fortunate that our company was purchased by responsible people. If you are careful when you select your buyer, you will have the same joy we feel, seeing the small business you created continue to thrive and benefit others.

Conclusions

I have described what we and other small business owners did that resulted in success. You will be successful too if you follow the advice given in this book. When you get started, you will probably have to moonlight, as we did. You may have to take a partner for a short time, as we did, or you may be a husband and wife team, as we were. Hopefully, you will use good advisors and consultants. Use them wisely, and remember your responsibilities both as buyer and as seller.

You know the importance of setting goals for yourself and your company and how they affect your quality standard, your employees, your customers, and your suppliers. You also know you can adapt or change goals, but you cannot lose sight of them.

One of the most important things you can do for yourself and your company is to promote it continually, with your banker, your investors, your customers, your suppliers, and your people. Never stop promoting your business. Focusing on those positive aspects of your business will help you successfully deal with disasters—those you bring on yourself and those that just happen.

Be sure you prepare for your company's success and your own, so that both you and your people benefit from that success, now and in the future.

Epilogue

Since selling our business, a number of people have asked us how things are going with the new owners. There is a belief, and much to support that belief, that when a small business owner sells to a large corporation, the employees are never treated as well, and the warmth and camaraderie that characterized the small business are lost. I am happy to report that the employees at our company are still enjoying all the benefits we established for them as co-founders and co-owners.

Luckily, I had developed my replacement so the manufacturing end of the business runs pretty much as it did when we were there. Naturally, each person brings his or her own management style to the job, so there are differences. But the major value system is still operating in our company. Employees still admit mistakes in order to produce a high quality product.

As I related in the Chapter 6, Gene's end of the business experienced a slight decline because the first new marketing director they hired was not effective. We helped the new owners find his replacement in addition to hiring an excellent marketing consultant. The business is, once again, prospering and growing.

We are proud of what we built. We believe others can do what we did by implementing the techniques for achieving success discussed in this book. If you decide to sell your business, we hope you are as fortunate as we were in finding the right buyer. If you are careful, you will be.

Index

Other Books of Interest

Business & Finance

Becoming Financially Sound in an Unsound World, $14.95

Careers in Child Care, $7.95

Cleaning Up for a Living: Everything You Need to Know to Become a Successful Building Service Contractor (2nd Ed.), $12.95

College Funding Made Easy: How to Save for College While Maintaining Eligibility for Financial Aid, $12.95

The Complete Guide to Buying and Selling Real Estate, $9.95

The Complete Guide to Buying Your First Home, $14.95

Doing Business in Asia, $18.95

Export-Import: Everything You and Your Company Need to Know to Compete in World Markets, $12.95

Homemade Money: The Definitive Guide to Success in a Homebased Business, $18.95

How to Make $100,000 a Year in Desktop Publishing, $18.95

How to Sell Your Home When Homes Aren't Selling, $16.95

How to Succeed as a Real Estate Salesperson: A Comprehensive Training Guide, $14.95

The Inventor's Handbook: How to Develop, Protect, & Market Your Invention, 2nd Ed., $12.95

Legal Aspects of Buying, Owning, and Selling a Home, $12.95

Little People, Big Business: A Guide to Successful In-Home Day Care, $7.95

People, Common Sense, and the Small Business, $9.95

Rehab Your Way to Riches: Guide to High Profit/Low Risk Renovation of Residential Property, $14.95

Single Person's Guide to Buying a Home: Why to Do It and How to Do It, $14.95

The Small Business Information Source Book, $7.95

Small Businesses That Grow and Grow and Grow, 2nd Ed., $9.95

Stay Home and Mind Your Own Business, $12.95

The Student Loan Handbook: All About the Stafford Loan Program and Other Forms of Financial Aid, 2nd Ed., $7.95

Surviving the Start-Up Years in Your Own Business, $7.95

Tradesmen In Business: A Comprehensive Guide and Handbook for the Skilled Tradesman, $14.95

Miscellaneous Reference

College Funding Made Easy: How to Save for College While Maintaining Eligibility for Financial Aid, $12.95

Cover Letters That Will Get You the Job You Want, $12.95

The First Whole Rehab Catalog: A Comprehensive Guide to Products and Services for the Physically Disadvantaged, $16.95

How to Handle the News Media, $7.95

The Insider's Guide to Buying a New or Used Car, $9.95

Making the Most of the Temporary Employment Market, $9.95

Speaking with Confidence: A Guidebook for Public Speakers, $7.95

For a complete catalog of Betterway Books write to the address below. To order, send a check or money order for the price of the book(s). Include $3.00 postage and handling for 1 book, and $1.00 for each additional book. Allow 30 days for delivery.

Betterway Books
1507 Dana Avenue, Cincinnati, Ohio 45207
Credit card orders call TOLL-FREE
1-800-289-0963
Quantities are limited; prices subject to change without notice.